7 TRUE TALES of TRIUMPH

CURATED BY: CHHAVII MEHTAA

AUTHORS:
CYRA ARORA | MANICKA KUMAR | RIA MEHTA
RUHANI VERMA | SAIRA MASTER KUMAR
SYNA AGGARWAL | YAMIA KHANNA

notionpress.com

INDIA · SINGAPORE · MALAYSIA

ISBN
Hardcase 979-8-89724-516-1
Paperback 979-8-89673-334-8

Contents

Acknowledgements

Writing the *7 True Tales of Triumph* has been a journey as profound and inspiring as the stories in it. This book is a tribute to the indomitable spirit of seven young individuals who dared to dream and persevered despite life's challenges. It was born out of a desire to inspire the youth of today by celebrating these seven true, resilient stories of young adults.

To my mom, my rock and guiding light—you are a source of inspiration and my cheerleader. Your wisdom, strength, and boundless love have been the bedrock of my life and this endeavour.

To my beloved children, Shaurya and Ria—you are the heart of my world and my greatest teachers. Through you, I've come to realise that parenting is not just about imparting knowledge, it's about learning and evolving alongside your children. You have taught me the true meaning of patience, resilience, and unconditional love. Through your innocence, you've shown me how to approach life with wonder and curiosity, how to embrace mistakes as a part of growth, and how to forgive, both others and myself. Both of you have helped me become a better parent, a better person, and a more compassionate coach. For all the lessons you've taught me, and for all the love you've shared, I am eternally thankful. You are, and will always be, my greatest teachers.

I extend my heartfelt gratitude to Anshu Arora, whose impressionable guidance, profound insights, and steadfast support have been the cornerstone of this book. Anshu, your vision about bringing these powerful themes to life, and your skill-building and ideation sessions along with compassionate hand-holding have helped these authors voice their thoughts and explore avenues they had not even visualised.

You have been the backbone of this journey and a pillar of strength. Your dedication has left an indelible mark on both the book and my heart.

From ideating with the authors to meticulously refining the details, your involvement has elevated this book to a level I couldn't have imagined. Your friendship and mentorship have been a true blessing, and I am grateful for your partnership throughout this journey.

My heartfelt thanks to Aditya Arya from Museo Camera, Centre for the Photographic Arts, for his generosity in supporting our seven young adults through his very specialised form of art—photography. A special thanks to Dinesh Khanna, whose incredible talent in profile photography added life to the front and back covers of the book. Dinesh Khanna is a professional photographer based in Gurugram and mainly shoots portraits, food, and interiors, besides travel.

I would also like to extend my gratitude to the talented illustrators, Vikrant Thakur and Eshita Arora, who spent time understanding each story to create an appropriate visual interpretation.

As they say, it takes a village to accomplish a humongous task like this. My gratitude to the parents of all the seven authors. Thank you for believing in this project. I appreciate the time and support you have given this book. This book is not a work of fiction; these are true stories of your children. I thank you for your exceptional parenting and for sharing the belief that these stories could inspire many others to follow the path your young star did.

Foreword

The 7 True Tales of Triumph is not just a book; it is a significant step towards acknowledging the spirit of youth. The life stories of these seven young adults highlight the 'never say die' spirit, the relentless search for the right path, and the unwavering commitment to following the righteous path of values.

The common thread throughout the book is that of grit, courage, and resilience.

I applaud the efforts of the mentor Ms. Chhavii Mehtaa and each of the seven girls who dared to follow and achieve their dreams.

Dr. Monika Kapoor
Founder and CEO, Skillshare India
Former Joint Director of CBSE

Introduction – The Allure of the Rising Sun

The dawn of a new day brings endless opportunities for those who dare to dream.

– Helen Keller

Chhavii Mehtaa, Curator

This simple truth is a powerful reminder that even when hidden by clouds, the sun will rise, ushering in the promise of a new day. The rising sun has always held a special fascination for me. Each day promises a fresh start, a clean slate, and the infinite potential to rise above yesterday's struggles. For me, as someone who works as a Teen Counsellor and Parenting Coach, it also symbolises the incredible resilience and energy that defines teenage—a phase of life brimming with possibilities, despite being clouded by challenges.

Young adults are much like the sun. They rise, shine, and light up the world around them. Each story in this book is a testament that despite facing turbulent family dynamics, societal pressures, or their own fears or failures, their spirits remain indomitable.

This anthology, the *7 True Tales of Triumph,* is a collection of true stories of those who dared to dream, stumbled but rose again, and achieved what seemed impossible. The process of ideation, writing, structuring, and showcasing this book gave me countless opportunities to revisit the world of teenagers. I was exposed to many new scenarios and challenges. However, what remained consistent was the spirit that defines this generation—to never give up, fight back, find the path, persevere, and most importantly, be authentic.

It wasn't all smooth sailing. There were conflicts, moments of self-doubt, and battles against societal expectations. But these challenges made their triumphs even more extraordinary.

Why This Anthology?

This book wasn't just a project; it was a calling. As someone who has worked closely with teenagers for years, I have experienced the magic of discovering potential firsthand.

But the idea for this anthology wasn't born overnight. I chose to take up this project because I believe in the power of stories to transform lives. Stories have a way of cutting through the noise and touching hearts. These narratives were not only meant to inspire the youth but also to act as a mirror for parents, educators, and mentors to understand their struggles and subsequent triumphs.

A Journey of Mentorship

As an educator, my philosophy (nurtured by my professional training and experience) is simple yet profound. I employ techniques like active listening, empathy, and personalised mentorship, always tailoring my approach to each child's unique needs.

My goal has always been to help the youth see the light within themselves. I strive to be a mirror, reflecting their strengths when they can't see them on their own.

Central to my work is the Japanese concept of ikigai, a sense of purpose that lies at the intersection of what a person loves, what they are good at, what the world needs, and what can sustain them. Discovering their ikigai means aligning their passions with their actions while being free from societal pressures.

As a mentor, this book gave me a chance to explore the spirit that defines this generation. What stood out was their unwavering resolve to overcome their struggles.

Through the process of writing this book, I witnessed the raw power of their determination. The resilience to rise after every fall, the ability to persevere through adversity, and the courage to stay true to oneself even in the face of judgement—these are the qualities that define the protagonists of these stories.

Stories of the Rising Sun

The seven stories featured in this book are a celebration of resilience and strength. Each story is a beacon of hope and a reminder of what young people can achieve when they believe in themselves and are given the right support.

You will see a marked difference in each story, despite the common threads. Some will be overly expressive and the others succinct and precise. I have made an intentional effort to let the flavour be governed by the personality of each author. I wanted you to meet the authors through their stories.

What This Book Taught Me

The process of writing and curating this book wasn't just about documenting these stories, it was a learning process.

One of the most profound lessons I learned is that resilience can be nurtured. With the right guidance, even the most daunting challenges can become stepping stones to success. I also realised, through the experiences quoted in the book, that failure is a necessary part of growth. As I often quote, "Every setback is a setup for a comeback."

The Allure of the Rising Sun: A Symbol of Hope

> *The rising sun sends its rays, soft and golden, piercing the haze of the morning, opening the world to all its possibilities.*

> **– Virginia Woolf**

This anthology is a celebration of the theme of the rising sun. The triumphs in this book are a tribute to the resilience, strength, and accomplishments of the seven young adults.

As you delve into these stories, I hope they inspire you to see the rising sun within yourself and those around you. Whether you are a teenager finding your way or an adult seeking to support the young people in your life, remember that every challenge is an opportunity to grow, and every setback is a setup for a comeback.

A Call to Action

To the readers, young adults, parents, teachers, and mentors reading this—let this book serve as a reminder of the incredible impact you can have on a young person's life. Your belief in them can be the light that guides them through the darkest times.

I would like the young adults of today to know that they are capable of incredible things. Your journey may be filled with challenges, but remember, the sun rises every day, and so can you. You can rise over your ordeals and tough situations and face the dawn of infinite possibilities.

I hope these stories encourage every reader to celebrate their own victories, big or small.

My Tryst with the 7 Tales

What drives young people to reach the peak of their potential? What pushes them to confront their deepest fears and to break free of the limitations society often places upon them? The answer lies not in a single trait but in the fusion of resilience, self-belief, and the courage to embrace the unknown. Each story in the *7 True Tales of Triumph* is a celebration of the extraordinary feats of young minds who, each in their unique way, have unlocked the key to their success. And the common thread? The relentless pursuit of growth, even in the face of fear.

While curating this book, I realised these stories are not mere anecdotes, but a reflection of the qualities that shape extraordinary lives. It is through this spirit that the journey becomes more important than the destination, and every triumph becomes a victory over the self. Life's most profound lessons often come not from reaching the destination but from the journey itself.

For 13-year-old Saira Master Kumar, a spirited adventurer with an insatiable curiosity for life, this truth is her guiding star.

Whether trekking to the awe-inspiring Everest Base Camp, mastering the discipline of martial arts, or carving her way down snowy slopes, Saira's life is a testament to perseverance, self-discovery, and the joy of living in the moment.

The journey of growth and transformation often unfolds in stages, each one adding depth and meaning to the bigger picture. Life is a masterpiece, and every experience is a brushstroke on its ever-evolving canvas. For Ruhani Verma, each colour was added while travelling from the darkest shades of personal illness to the vibrant hues of experiential learning imparted by the four prominent people in her life. These were lessons of resilience, self-discovery, humility, and intentional living.

However, it is not only in achievements that we find success. Success comes from the ability to champion life skills that directly impact how one manages emotions, makes decisions, and accepts the areas of improvement. It is also about the ability to leave behind the familiar and embrace the unknown. For 15-year-old Cyra Arora, stepping into the demanding world of a boarding school was not just a change of scenery but a bold leap into self-transformation. Her journey began from the moment she walked into the principal's office for an intense interview. It was not one of ease but of courage, resilience, and the relentless pursuit of growth.

This idea of transformation is beautifully echoed in Syna Aggarwal's melodic journey. Her journey is much like the bamboo tree that grows resiliently beneath the surface before bursting into its full glory above. Beginning her musical exploration at the age of eight, Syna's love for music was never a fleeting pursuit, it was her life's purpose.

Manicka Kumar's story is a powerful testament to the human spirit's ability to rise above self-doubt and emotional turbulence. From moments of questioning her place in the world to finding the courage to create her magnum opus, her journey is one of resilience, transformation, and the pursuit of meaning.

Yamia Khanna's journey is a powerful reminder that true boldness isn't just about strength, it is about embracing vulnerability and cultivating empathy. It is also about learning from observing. Through personal challenges and moments of self-doubt, Yamia discovered that courage lies not in the absence of fear but in facing it with resilience and compassion.

And it is this courage that forms the backbone of Ria Mehta's journey. In a world often dominated by noise—external judgements, societal pressures, and doubts—Ria's journey offers a rare and profound lesson in stillness. Inspired by the quiet strength of her grandfather, a man who weathered life's storms with grace, she uncovered the art of 'noise cancellation,' filtering out negativity to focus on her true self.

Together, these seven stories teach us that the path to triumph is not a straight line; it is a winding journey full of bumps, detours, and moments of doubt. Yet it is through the will to continue, the courage to embrace imperfection, and the willingness to transform our setbacks into strengths that these young adults have achieved greatness. The *7 True Tales of Triumph* isn't just a book about victories—it is a celebration of the journey itself, a reminder that it's the grit, the courage, and the unyielding commitment to our values that lead us to triumph.

Meet the Authors

Saira Master Kumar   **Ruhani Verma**

Cyra Arora   **Syna Aggarwal**   **Manicka Kumar**

Yamia Khanna   **Ria Mehta**

TRUE TALE 1

IT'S ALWAYS THE JOURNEY, NEVER THE DESTINATION

SAIRA MASTER KUMAR

It's Always the Journey, Never the Destination

When I told my friends and family that I had finished the Everest Base Camp (EBC) Trek, they all looked at me with awe. My grandmothers, uncles, and aunts congratulated me, and friends looked at me with admiration.

"Wow!" they all said, "Saira, how brave you are!"

Not brave. Not at all. No one knows the facts, the behind-the-scenes (BTS) scenarios that actually happened. If I had to make a video of the BTS of the trek, videos that my friends love to watch, it would show you another picture altogether! I was anything but brave. I was tired, cold, wet and hungry, and that's the unfiltered, candid, unscripted truth! I love reality shows like Dubai Bling, but my mom tells me that they're all scripted and made for television. Well, my trek to EBC was anything but that! And yet, there was drama, emotion, blood, sweat, and tears—I swear!

In this chapter, I am going to try and share the BTS of my life with you. The BTS of my accolades and achievements and what truly matters to me—the plain, honest, and real truth!

So, let us start with me.

My name is Saira, and I'm an outgoing and positive person who is very fond of the outdoors. This doesn't mean I'm not into fashion and makeup; it just means I have balanced preferences.

Out of everything I have done so far in my 13 years, and everything I have achieved, I never thought being called a published author would be one of them! My treks, medals in sports, progress in martial arts, being the fastest downhill skier among my friends—all of this makes me look strong and confident, but there is a lot going on BTS and I am here to share that with you!

I don't like to boast like a self-obsessed person, yet, I must tell you about some of my recent achievements.

Firstly, I went on and completed the 16-day EBC Trek. I am now practising for my black belt in Karate, which I will hopefully get next year. Did I tell you I have learned four different styles of martial arts? But wait, I am moving too fast. I play tennis and soccer and have a hard time choosing between the two, I must admit.

If you have digested all of this, then let me push in a little more.

I was never keen on going to the EBC. Even if it meant that I was the rare 12-year-old in my group to achieve it (my thirteenth birthday was still two months away!)

Honestly, achieving something has never been my intent. I just love the 'doing' part. Whether I won or lost, reached the base camp or not, it never mattered. For me, what really mattered was my love for sports and showing great sportsmanship while at it. And staying humble. I think staying humble is really important. Because there will always be someone better than me in whatever I do. For me, it's about how I improve and how I show it—to myself.

Whether it is trekking, martial arts, skiing, tennis or soccer, I just like to take things one step at a time. I enjoy the process, more than the achievement or the destination. I learned that from my father.

I remember, when I was five years old and we were driving in the mountains, I had asked my dad, "Have we reached yet?"

And his answer always was, "Yes! Look around you, we're where we want to be!" Even if 'around me' meant just a long, empty, winding mountain road with nothing nearby!

For me, everything is a part of a checklist. I finish one thing and then go on to the next, checking things off as I go along. When each task is finished, I enjoy my much-needed victory! It is this mindset that truly helped me in getting through the EBC Trek. We climbed up the never-ending steps to Namche Bazaar. The steps were tall, muddy, and full of scree, and the route was exceptionally long! Each step felt like ten! I took them on, literally a step at a time until I finally reached the top. There must have been at least a thousand steps! Are you doing the math about multiplying each step with ten yet?

Yes, I finally did reach the EBC, but do you want to know the real truth, the BTS story? Here goes. The day we were to reach the base camp, we started from our lodge at 0400 hours. It was dark outside. All the water had turned to ice and crunched beneath my feet as I walked. The temperature was around – 15ºC and both my mind and body were confused. The water in my water bladder pipe was frozen too, and yet there was sweat pouring down my face. I wasn't feeling hot, but neither was I cold. From the top of my head to the bottom of my toes, I was just numb and sweating. Sweating as if I were in the Sahara Desert! And to add to it all, I was hungry!

The packed sandwich in my bag was frozen stiff, and there was no way I could eat it. Same with the apple, it was hard as stone.

"Wait for the sun to rise," my mommy said, "Let's move fast, away from this mountain range so the sun can reach us."

Mom would know! She was the trek leader, and she'd done this trek so many times.

She said, "See, that's Pumori, and look, that's Nuptse. Isn't she beautiful?"

Frankly, I wasn't interested. I just wanted to move away from these mountains so I could feel the sun. It was rising slowly, hiding behind the tall 7000 m peaks surrounding us. I was cold, I was hot, I was hungry! The confusion and anxiety overwhelmed me, leading to a flood of tears that seemed endless.

And then I realised, this wouldn't make my problems go away, it would just make them worse. And so, I kept walking. And with each step I took, the closer I was to finally being at peace. Step by step, with thousands more to go, I reached the EBC. It was the best victory I could have asked for!

We were accompanied on the trek by our guides—Chrin, Dawa Dai, and Dolma. I observed how resilient they were, always smiling, laughing, ever helpful. While I sat sipping my well-deserved piping hot cocoa (which felt like heaven!), I realised how privileged I was. This trek and this journey was a choice for me. I chose to be here (kicking and screaming a little, I must admit). But the guides didn't have an option. For them, it was a mandate; it was their job. This made me appreciate my lifestyle much more. What I did for my enjoyment, thrill, and passion was bread and butter for them!

Dawa, Chrin and Dolma became my best friends on the trek. Dolma was just 21 years old. She was closest to my age, the others were double or even triple my age! She told me how she wanted to be a trekking guide just like her father. Dawa Dai was an Everester; he had summited the Everest twice already and talked to me about his home and family back in the village. I told him how much I loved shopping, and he's now keen on coming to Delhi to go shopping with me!

Chrin was our chief guide and he became everyone's best friend on the trek. He had the happiest, most positive personality, and he never fumbled when it came to ordering food for me! If someone forgot their walking stick or walked up ahead too fast, it was one of the guides who would run back to grab the stick or run forward to catch up, sometimes climbing those steps and that trail twice over, while I huffed and puffed all the way to do it just once!

I made friends with all the older people on the trek too. Though I walked faster than most of them, they took the time to chat with me when we all caught up at lunch points and later in the evening at the lodge. It was these friends that really helped make the trek a memorable one and worth the 16 days of my summer holidays! The memories and experiences I had on the way, that is what I will always remember, along with the wonderful people I met on the journey. In many ways, the trek changed my life; it showed me a different side of the world I had lived in up to now and introduced me to the different people who helped make this world a better place to live in. I realise now that it was never about reaching the EBC.

I now understand what my father always tried to teach me when he said, "We're where we want to be!" always emphasising the journey and enjoying it.

My other teacher was Shifu Kanishk, India's only Shaolin Master. "Focus, Saira," he would always say. "Stay focused."

I started learning Kung Fu with him when I was just five years old. Now, after eight years of martial arts, I think I'm pretty experienced if I say so myself! I learned not one or two but three different types of martial arts—Shaolin Kung Fu, Muay Thai, and two styles of Karate.

BTS fact: In these eight years of learning, I have been hurt, badly bruised, and even had a bleeding nose. In all this, there were two golden rules I remembered, and listen to me carefully when I say this: the first one is 'A tear won't fix your problems.'

In all my experiences, I am reminded more than once, that whether it is trekking or sports, everyone has problems and struggles. What people face BTS no one ever knows. All of us face problems, and our problems appear very difficult to us, but there is always someone fighting a bigger battle or trying to complete a more difficult race.

In Kung Fu, Shifu would make me kick a wooden log to build more strength. I learned to keep my legs stretched up high. In Karate, I did burpees and push-ups until my hands were numb. And what have I learned from all this? I now know that 'whatever I do, I must do with focus.' That if I really wanted something, shedding tears and crying about the struggles involved weren't going to get me anywhere, only focus would.

So, I worked hard, and every time we shifted cities, I started learning a new martial art because, for me, giving up wasn't an option. The second golden rule I learned from martial arts, and stay with me while I say this, is: 'Shut up and show up.'

From Kung Fu to Karate to Muay Thai, that is the one important thing I have learned. Whatever happens, just show up. The rest of it will take care of itself. I follow the Okinawa Shorin Ryu style of Karate, and my dojo is in Bangalore now, and I will soon start training for my black belt. I love martial arts, and while tournaments are fun and a great way for me to gauge my level, it's not why I do them. I just like getting out in the open air. That's the honest truth.

Open spaces and the great outdoors have always been an option for me. It's something I have often taken for granted. I've been trekking since I was four, and I never really appreciated all the mountains and valleys I got to go to, until now.

Delhi was where my childhood was spent and who doesn't like revisiting lovely old memories? Now that I live in Bengaluru, I miss my Delhi days. But earlier this year, when I visited my home in Delhi, I got sick to the point where it was difficult to breathe. I was put on a nebuliser and inhalers and told to rest as there were signs of asthma.

It was hard dealing with my asthma, knowing the number of sports I participated in. Every breath felt like my lungs were working double time to simply breathe. I could almost visualise the black smoky gases and fumes released in Delhi entering my trachea and slowly making their way to my lungs, and once they reached there, they were like germs contaminating my whole body. It was hard dealing with this. It also helped me appreciate the great outdoors that I had taken for granted until now.

Instead of whining and complaining about the enforced rest, I just waited it out. Three months later, I went for the EBC Trek and oh, what a lung detox that was! I was breathless walking uphill and downhill and sometimes chasing the shy, rainbow-coloured Himalayan Monal across the moraine, but it was the best kind of breathlessness! I could feel the difference. I wasn't out of breath because of the pollution in Delhi or the pollen in Bangalore; it was due to my running around, cuddling little puppies on the trail, finding a hot chocolate stand, or even a café that served the most delicious apple pie!

I've come to realise that the mountain air has an earthy taste. The crisp morning air has an unmatched flavour, and it's a gift, a much-needed gift for my lungs—one that I will never, ever take for granted again. And do you know what else gives me that feeling? Skiing down a mountain slope! The icy wind hits my face, and it seems like the whole mountain is just for me. It's just me, the mountains, the sky, and nothing else. It's the most awesome feeling in the world! My father taught me skiing when I was three and a half years old. I have memories of standing on my little skis, safely between his own, sliding down a mountain slope harnessed firmly to a rope he held. To this day, skiing is my favourite sport. My father was India's national champion in downhill speed skiing, and my aunt (his sister) represented India in the Calgary Olympics in 1988. But I have never been interested in competing. I just want to enjoy my skiing journey. I have fallen many times, hurt my wrists, got stuck knee-deep in snow, and been slammed by a speed skier too—that's the BTS story of my skiing. But I learned to get up and ski again every time.

Skiing doesn't make me feel boxed in or contained, like tennis or soccer, where there are rules to follow, or where I have to play within the lines. I simply want to feel that freedom and enjoy that whizz down the mountainside without having to win anything.

Got to admit though, I don't feel the same way about tennis and football! There, I play to win! Strange, no? Maybe it's because I'm playing for a team and not just myself. I have played tennis for seven years now and football for two. As much as I love both, they do end up tiring me out. I am on both the tennis and football teams for my school and go to many inter-school tournaments, which makes it all worth it.

The truth though? The BTS reality? All this comes at a cost. Two hours of tennis, four days a week, and then football three times a week, not including the other extracurriculars. It is exhausting. But I have been improving and my days are long. But, like in Karate, I suit up and show up. That's what I do, and this helps me to stay on the teams, play for my academy, and win. I hope to get on the state team for football by continuing to use this method.

Sometimes I am confused. What do I love more? Sports or animals? And do I really need to choose? I have rescued more animals than I have done homework assignments, and that's God's own truth! Oreo has been my favourite rescue of all time. An abused puppy, she was tied up with a chain behind our home in Goa. I would come back from school every day, only to see her hungry and thirsty, and the chain barely let her move. She would whine when she saw me from afar, and her white miserable tail would begin to wag slowly, almost hopefully. One day, I could not resist it anymore and I broke the chain with a stone. Oreo couldn't believe she was free. She sat up, wagged her tail and whined, ever so quietly.

"Shh…" I said, "Don't cry, or he'll wake up!"

And then I ran! I ran for my life because I was scared that Oreo's owner, a drunk, would come chasing after me! And trusting me,

Oreo followed all the way home. Of course, my mom ranted and raved and then dished out a meal of chicken broth and bread because she thought, "Let's feed her before we send her back!"

I named her Oreo because, yes, you guessed it, she had one black eye patch and the other side was white! She was only one month old, a skinny white-and-black creature that was raised on jalebis from the nearby temple. Often, the old drunk man would scream from the other side of the wall that he wanted his dog back, but I never gave in.

I took care of Oreo for nine months—bathed her, removed her ticks, got her the vaccinations she needed, and also arranged for her sterilisation. She was a free, happy dog who appeared magically, bounding joyfully, whenever I shouted, "Oreeee!" from my terrace!

Oreo was a crazy girl! Just like me! She and I had a bond like no other. Ah no, I lie. There was one other rescue that was just as magical. Three little bulbuls were found by a tree in our garden. The mother was nowhere to be found and the nest had obviously fallen from the tree. I managed to save two of them. Every morning and evening, I would feed them with cotton wool soaked in milk or chicken soup. They grew stronger every day until they began to trot out of the little cage I had made for them, all on their own! And my biggest achievement? I taught them to fly! Yes! I would put them on the tips of my fingers and shake my hand and body up and down until they fluttered their little wings. It was just so unreal! And then one day, one of them took a short flight and landed on the grass, about five feet away from me. I was the mamma bird! I had taught them to fly!

When it was time for us to move out of Goa, I cried for hours, knowing I had to leave all this behind. We handed Oreo over to our house help, who loved her too, and I knew she would be taken care of. This experience showed me that nothing lasts forever, so we should just enjoy the moments while they're here. Just enjoy the journey, you know? It doesn't always have to be about getting somewhere.

Someone once told me a story about a lady who had to carry a bucket of water up and down a hill every day. But the bucket had a hole, and by the time she reached the top, she had only half the water left. To her amazement, after a few months, the path she had taken every day was filled with flowers!

And so is my journey. Achievements and outcomes have never been my goals. I've found that the experiences, the 'flowers' that I have gathered, are far more enthralling than any 'win' or 'victory.' If those were my only goals, my stories would be short and boring, but I make sure that the journey is always fun. And I have made many friends, both human and furry, to help me make this journey memorable and happy.

As Confucius said, "The way is the goal." And I have thoroughly enjoyed my way, all along.

I have consolidated my life's lessons in a journal. I keep going back to it during moments of introspection or whenever I feel a reminder is much needed.

Each lesson has a page. Let me share a glimpse of the titles of some pages.

Title 1: Stay humble

Title 2: Enjoy the process (I am a natural at this!)

Title 3: A tear won't fix your problems! (Experience this every day, through all the tough moments of practice and prep)

Title 4: Shut up and show up! (Believe me, it takes an external force to make this happen!) and lastly,

Title 5: It does not have to be about getting somewhere! (This is the one I go back to the most!)

So there you see, that's the BTS of my life. I want to remind you to keep looking at the BTS of your lives, just like I do through my journal. Look carefully, is it filled with joy or not? Are you having fun while you do what you do? I realised while reading this that I find joy, not in finishing an activity, but in just doing it.

I'm not saying that the destination is irrelevant, or less important. But so often, in worrying about reaching the destination, we forget to enjoy the journey. The 'getting there' part is every bit as important to me as arriving at the destination. I have learned to appreciate people, animals, birds, experiences—everything! I have learned to appreciate my privileges and the difficulties. And I am only 13, so I am sure many more adventures and experiences are waiting for me. There are many such BTS to be played, watched, and experienced. I am ready to embrace it all with an open mind and a warm, humble heart. All I need is the hot chocolate at the end of it!

Saira Master is a 13-year-old adventurer with a love for sports, animals, and open skies. From reaching the Everest Base Camp to teaching baby birds to fly and rescuing stray pups, she believes in taking life one step at a time. Her philosophy: "Let the journey teach you more than the destination."

TRUE TALE 2

THE PRISM AND THE CANVAS

RUHANI VERMA

TRUE TALE 2

The Prism and the Canvas

Salvador Dalí, the master of surrealism, was known not only for his strikingly bizarre art but also for his peculiar quirks. One of his most intriguing habits was taking ultra-short power naps—holding a key above a metal plate and letting its clang wake him just as he drifted into unconsciousness. He described his art as 'hand-painted dream photographs,' blending awkwardness with genius to craft works uniquely his own.

Like Dalí, we all possess peculiarities, awkward yet essential traits that define our identities. Each life, with its strokes of experience, creates a unique canvas, telling a story only its creator can paint. My canvas may not rival Dalí's or da Vinci's, but it is mine, shaped by every awkward detail, every hue of emotion, and every unspoken story.

When you enter my room, it will be faintly scented with paint thinner and the air will be thick with the mingling aromas of acrylic and possibility. I love how a brush dances across the canvas—erratic and undefined, yet purposeful.

A thought crosses my mind, "Life is like a paint palette."

Each stroke of experience, every hue of observation, and the spectrum of unsettling emotions blend to create a unique canvas. The colours don't always have to be bright; they can be dark, intense, faint, or bold. Together, they form a masterpiece in progress.

But my canvas wasn't always so vivid. Growing up, I wasn't the child who noticed the little things. I moved through life lost in my own rhythm, rarely pausing. Then, without warning, came the unknown—a diagnosis of tuberculosis, followed by surgery, and medication. A seven-year friendship ended. These events stripped me of certainty, forcing me to pause and look around. This pause was transformative. The enthusiastic, jumpy version of me began noticing the world anew, as if through a prism that splits light into countless colours.

I recalled Ferris Bueller's words, "Life moves pretty fast. If you don't stop and look around occasionally, you could miss it."

I had been moving too fast. Life doesn't make complete sense because we lack the completeness to grasp it (from Brian Hines' Life is Fair). Could our limited view of existence obscure life's lessons? Fleeting encounters began to carry profound meaning. I learned to appreciate small efforts and the warmth they brought—a stranger's selflessness, the effect of a smile, or the resilience of a stray dog.

These experiences were brushstrokes, adding empathy, resilience, and kindness to my palette. Each moment taught me something new, enriching the masterpiece of my life.

Looking back, I realise this journey began with my Papa and his art of composure and problem-solving. I've seen him remain unshaken during life-threatening challenges. I vividly remember our short car rides home from my math tuition. In those few minutes, I would pour out my worries. Without fail, Papa would provide thoughtful solutions, leaving me in awe of his calmness.

One memory stands out. I woke abruptly, one early morning, sensing something was off. I was stirred awake by a silence I couldn't fathom—a quiet nudge from the depths of my intuition, pulling me from sleep as if the universe had something urgent to say. As I woke up from the gentle tumbles of my warm quilt, I was surprised to find my sister in the exact same position as me—both of us staring at each other in the stillness. Something felt off. We rushed to our parents' room, only to find it empty. Panic crept in as we realised no one in the house knew where they were and their phones went unanswered. At 0746 hours, my sister's phone finally rang.

My mom's voice trembled on the other end, laced with despair, as she stuttered that their factory had caught fire, destroying a substantial portion of the completed shipment due to be sent out soon. The loss was immense. The rest of us grieved openly, our voices heavy with sorrow, as if the world paused to feel our pain. Each word felt like a release of grief, pressing down on our hearts like a stone.

While we grieved openly, Papa remained composed. Instead of dwelling on the problem, he channelled his energy into finding solutions. What struck me the most was his response to the worker who had accidentally forgotten to turn off the switch to the press, leading to the fire. Papa went up to him and, to my surprise, hugged him. He chose forgiveness over blame, handling the situation with such quiet dignity that he never mentioned the incident again to the worker or anyone else.

That moment taught me true strength isn't about facing challenges head-on; it's about how we respond when everything crumbles.

I remember a time when my anger would often spiral out of control. Pillows would be thrown, one after another, till they were scattered all over the floor—my frustration spilling over, my anger unchecked. This one time, after throwing all the pillows, I saw my dad picking them up.

And a thought crossed my mind, "Why did I do that? It didn't even make sense."

So, I went up to him and asked him, "How do I control my anger?"

Papa thought for a moment, then came up with the funniest and strangest advice.

"Whenever you feel angry, just start studying incessantly."

I thought, "What does that even mean?"

And laughed it off, dismissing it as another one of his quirky ideas. But over time, as I observed him, I began to understand. I watched how he remained calm and composed, even in the most difficult situations. Slowly, I learned to control my anger.

Looking back, I realise the power of pausing. If Papa hadn't paused that day, if he had fired the worker, shouted at the factory staff, or cried with us, everything would have unravelled differently. But he hadn't. Instead, he had paused. He had listened. He had observed. He had watched. I know he had said his prayers and expressed his gratitude, thanking the Lord for the other million things that were spared in the accident.

Papa's resilience influenced me deeply, but as I grew more reflective, I realised my Mumma was shaping me too. While Papa exemplified composure, Mumma demonstrated love, balance, and tireless dedication. The word to be emphasised here is TIRELESS. She didn't always wear her emotions as gracefully as he did. Her expressions were raw and her worries were more visible. But it was in her vulnerability and relentless efforts that I discovered another layer of life's opportunity. She worked late into the night, even when pregnant, lifting boxes of shipment while balancing family life with grace. Back then, when my parents were low on staff and struggling to establish themselves, Mumma worked late into the night, sometimes till 0300 hours, managing operations with an unyielding spirit. Yet, despite the gruelling hours, her presence was felt and her love was known.

My mother's ability to juggle so much while giving so much of herself with such kindness amazed me. What stood out, besides everything being perfectly in place, was her passion and ambition. Her unwavering compassion and ability to create harmony, even in chaos, were remarkable.

She loved everyone around her with genuine care, even those who may have wronged her. No matter the situation, she treated everyone with more kindness than necessary. It's inspiring how she remained true to her values and unshaken in her integrity.

I remember her telling me, "Bunny, jhuke hue paedho par hee phal ugte hain." (The tree laden with fruits always bends low.)

If you wish to be great, be kind and humble. This is something her father used to tell her. She would calm my somewhat opinionated self by explaining that a fruit-bearing tree bends low, while one without fruits stands upright. Pride and ego prevent others from benefiting, while humility shows that a person has something to offer.

Her lessons in humility shaped me. I remember a time when I needed some help from a friend. I had missed a few classes and had asked if I could borrow her notes, but to my surprise, she had refused. I wasn't very happy about it, in fact, I was a little annoyed. I couldn't understand why she wouldn't help me with something so small, but I decided to let it go and not dwell on it.

Some time passed, and the tables turned. She came to me, needing help herself. This time, she wanted to borrow a book for an assignment, and when she asked me, I could feel the weight of the decision I had to make.

A part of me thought, "Why should I help her when she didn't help me?"

But then, I remembered something my Mumma always said, "No matter what anyone else does, you have to stay true to your own values."

Her words echoed in my mind, and I realised this was one of those moments where I could choose who I wanted to be. So, I set aside my annoyance and decided to help her.

I must admit, it wasn't easy or magical. I had to stop the words, "No, I can't," and then consciously make space for, "Sure!"

Though it took some effort, I did it. Sometimes, handing over a book could also be a challenge to overcome if you are trying to stick to certain values and are committed to their application in life.

Another cornerstone of my learning was my sister or my Didi.

It was my Didi who taught me the true meaning of courage— standing up for yourself and your beliefs, even when it's tough.

She's my mirror and guide, always giving me the strength to stand firm. She never hesitates to speak her mind or confront someone when she sees something wrong. When my life's momentum slows, she's the catalyst that energises me.

She is one of the strongest people I know, not just emotionally, but in every sense. She's the part of my heart that, despite the miles between us, remains the most important. During her 12th board exams, when the pressure was high and everyone had their opinions, our parents favoured the traditional route of tuition and extra classes. But Didi believed in self-study and the guidance of her school teachers. She trusted her own system, one that allowed her to focus on what was most important.

Despite our parents' concerns, Didi remained steadfast in her decision. It wasn't easy; even mom stopped talking to her for a while, struggling to understand why Didi wouldn't follow her advice. But Didi believed in herself and didn't let doubts or external pressures sway her.

The result? She got impeccable scores, surpassing even her own convictions and instincts, even when everyone else disagreed.

Watching Didi follow her instincts taught me valuable lessons. She would often say, "Intuition doesn't tell you what you want to hear; it tells you what you need to hear."

Her belief in herself and her system, and her refusal to back down showed me that strength lies in trusting your own path.

I learned that standing up for your beliefs with complete conviction brings clarity and resolution. Slowly, I began to emulate her, realising that avoiding problems only delays growth. By accepting and confronting our weaknesses, we can begin the journey towards improvement. Didi taught me the art of turning avoidance into action.

Finally, the fourth reflection in the prism of my life was my best friend Disha, who gave me the courage to apologise. Her ability to prioritise relationships over pride inspired me. Though initially uncomfortable with saying 'sorry,' I learned its power in mending bonds. With Disha, I realised true friendships thrive on understanding and care, not just apologies.

Though I moved out of my family home, Disha has always remained a part of my inner circle. She taught me an entirely different kind of courage—the courage to let go of my ego and apologise. I dare say this was the toughest lesson and the biggest learning!

Disha's actions always proved to me that, "If you have one true friend, you have more than your share."

She is the sweetest person in any room, and her kindness shines through everything she does. There was a time when saying 'sorry' felt impossible for me, almost like an insurmountable obstacle. The authentic apology and I were never friends. I struggled with it because of my ego, vulnerability, and even a lack of empathy. I'll admit, the word made me uncomfortable—until Disha helped me understand its true meaning.

I was trapped by my ego, too proud to say the simplest of words to mend what was broken. Disha taught me that an apology isn't just a word—it's an invisible thread that connects two souls and repairs what pride has shattered.

She made me realise that sorry is an easy word. Disha values the people she loves deeply, and no matter the disagreement, if she felt the fight had strayed from what truly mattered, she would apologise first. For her, protecting the bond was more important than protecting her pride. She never waited to be told she'd hurt someone – if she thought she'd offended anyone, she'd go out of her way to make it right.

"I just don't want anyone to feel hurt because of me," she'd say, brushing it off like it was no big deal. But to me, it was everything.

Her ability to sense when someone is down, sometimes before they even know it, is something I admire about her profoundly. Over time, though, I began to notice something else—Disha apologised a lot, even for the smallest things, even when it wasn't needed. It became such a habit that I decided to intervene—not because I didn't value her kindness, but because I didn't want her to feel responsible for everyone else's emotions.

One day, I made a pact with her, and said, "From now on, you're not allowed to say sorry for the little things. You already apologise to everyone, even when it's unnecessary. With me, no more unnecessary apologies. Deal?"

She laughed and tried to protest, but eventually, she agreed. And though she slipped up now and then, it became our rule. It was my way of reminding her that her kindness didn't always need to be followed by an apology—sometimes, just being herself was enough.

Disha taught me that while apologies can mend bonds, true friendships don't always need them. They thrive on understanding, forgiveness, and the simple pact to always be there for each other. She inspired me to care a little more, be a little kinder, and love a lot more with every passing day.

There's a day that still lingers in my memory like an unfinished brushstroke. One soft morning, I arrived at my tuition and noticed a dog crying with its face stuck in the door. A few of us tried to help, but when our math teacher arrived, he told us to go inside, assuring us that his assistant would handle it. Reluctantly, I sat down, thinking it was out of my hands.

But one boy stayed behind. While the rest of us moved on, he waited, determined to help the dog until it was free. Watching him, I realised how rare and beautiful it is to pause and care deeply when the world urges you to move on. I could have dismissed this moment as just another fleeting scene, but it stayed with me. It reminded me that sometimes, choosing to pause and observe is the first step towards truly making a difference. I could have dismissed the moment as just another fleeting scene in the tapestry of life. But instead, I chose to pause. To observe. To absorb.

It is not just pausing—the key differentiator lies in what happens next. All of us were faced with the same situation, and all of us paused, but only one of us acted. That moment of pausing was an opportunity for reflection, but the game-changer was how it was interpreted and translated into action. We all had the same chance to make a difference, yet only one person chose to act. Everyone paused, but not everyone converted that pause into meaningful action. That boy turned his contemplation into a decision that positively impacted someone else's life. This is the essence of change—how we translate passion into action, how we transform a pause into purpose. And it's not just about one isolated act; it's about consistency. It's about picking up the brush repeatedly, creating not just one painting but many, each filled with purpose and intent.

If I am passionate about something but never pick up the brush, there will never be a painting on the canvas. Ambition and knowledge mean little if they are not acted upon. Without action, I risk killing a thousand ideas before they even see the light of day. Next time, I want to be the one who frees the dog! The passion I absorb, and the lessons I learn—they shouldn't end at reflection. They demand action, because only action can bring those ideas to life and create a real, lasting impact.

Life's most profound lessons often come from its quietest moments. We learn not just by seeing but by absorbing and letting those random strokes of experience blend into our canvas. And when we observe with a certain intent, we discover that every challenge, every fleeting encounter, and every random stroke has the potential to teach us resilience, compassion, or courage.

Pause. Observe. Absorb. Act. And that's how I continue to paint the canvas of my life.

Each of these four figures, through the prism of their love, humility, resilience, and courage, has reflected hues on the canvas of my life—hues I never knew I needed.

Ruhani Verma is a 17-year-old with a curious mind and a deep love for innovation and the natural world. She finds inspiration in the world around her, from the colours of a sunset to the patterns in nature. Always curious, Ruhani loves to observe and learn, believing that each step forward holds valuable lessons. Her philosophy: "Art is not just what you see, but what you feel and learn from every moment."

•••

TRUE TALE 3

AND THE MOON SAID, "YOU DON'T HAVE TO BE WHOLE TO SHINE"

CYRA ARORA

TRUE TALE 3

And the Moon Said, "You Don't Have to Be Whole to Shine"

"The heights by great men reached and kept
Were not attained by sudden flight,
But they, while their companions slept,
Were toiling upward in the night."

– Henry Wadsworth Longfellow

The words of Henry Wadsworth truly define the choice I made at 14 years of age—to go to a boarding school, a path that is not normally taken by many teenagers.

It all started with an interview, one that would make me learn a new way of being and explore a new life. My mind was racing faster than an F1 car on the racetrack. My heart was fluttering and everything was blurry. When I was about to go for my interview with the principal of the boarding school, despite all the time that I had spent reading and understanding about it, I felt I was not prepared at all. I felt like a mess. I had never felt so nervous before!

To me, the wooden door with the metal plate that read 'Principal's Office' was scarier than a horror movie! My parents pushed me into the room and there he was, sitting in his chair—Principal Sir! Dressed formally in a suit and tie, he extended his hand for a handshake. I shook his hand firmly and sat on the chair right across the table.

He started talking casually about my interests and achievements and then asked me about the meaning of my name, Cyra.

"I have heard this name, but have never seen this spelling before," he said.

I replied, "It has Parsi origins and my name means Moon, God's gift or God sent. Yes, sure, it's not common and I love that!"

After learning about this, he gave me a sheet of paper and a pen and asked me to write a story using the three words—Moon, God's gift and God sent. What? I was not prepared for this. This wasn't even in the syllabus!

Nevertheless, I took it in my stride. I wrote something that implied, 'The moon is the most beautiful God's gift to the sky. It shines most beautifully through the night, changing many faces. The moon looks different throughout the year. It is absolutely beautiful in all its forms. However, the beautiful moon, with its many spots, is also imperfect. Despite its scars, it is considered the most beautiful creation of God.'

As I showed this piece to him, he said, "I must add that the other beautiful God's gift, as beautiful as the moon, is Cyra, who is God sent to her parents. She too is loved despite her imperfections."

On that emotional note, we struck a bond and he said to my parents, "Now you are not seeking admission for this child, I am seeking this child from you." That moment marked the beginning of my journey.

After taking a round of the school and agreeing to join it, I came back home and started mentally preparing myself to expect and experience new things. Well, you don't know me yet. Since you're embarking on this journey with me as I narrate it, it's only fair that you get to know me first. Allow me to introduce myself.

I am a 15-year-old who likes to sketch, listen to music, and play sports. I like talking to new people and making new friends. I also like to annoy my parents and friends, just for fun! My most cherished trait is that I am happy most of the time! That should give you a basic idea about me.

You should also know about the 7-year-old me. A little girl with a broken front tooth who made it into the India Book of Records for skating.

But back to my journey. Let me pick it up from where I left off earlier. A few weeks passed after the interview with the principal and D-day arrived! I am sure you would have guessed the obvious. Yes, my parents were more nervous about dropping me at the school than I was about starting this new chapter. Throughout the car ride, my mom and dad were offering me advice that I had heard a million times before. So instead of anxiety, I was bored and started feeling sleepy!

We reached my room at the hostel, unpacked, and then it was time for my parents to bid adieu to me. And from that moment on, my experiences began. By that, I mean the fun part of being alone with friends, enjoying every day and, may I say, no problems? Yay!

On the first day, I made two or three friends. And on the second day, there was a cycling trip. We cycled for 10 km that day, but I do not remember it as cycling was fun. I fell into a mud pit just because my feet could barely touch the ground. I made a fool of myself and put myself in an embarrassing position right on the second day of school.

The actual classes began the following day, and so did the infamous morning PT. It was the worst form of torture imaginable!

"Cyra, when will you get used to this?" I asked myself.

I've come to realise that morning PT and evening sports are never, and will never be, fun! After a few months, I accepted my fate and stopped trying to skip the morning PT.

Life at the boarding school was filled with fun and drama. So technically, you didn't have to pay for a Netflix subscription because the events in your life will be nothing short of a comedy show with endless episodes.

Within the first few days of joining the boarding school, I was asked, "Cyra, you must be missing your family, friends and home!"

Me? Missing someone? Hell, nah! I was enjoying my life alone, and with my friends by my side, doing all things fun! On the other hand, my parents were very worried about me, which made it even funnier (well!). It is not that I like to see my parents worry, it's just that I love their overly expressive reactions. I love it! They are simply priceless!

As I write this, I know that I will always remember the first room I lived in—room no. 3 (my lucky number); my first class: IX B; my first roommates: Zoya, Li, Prisini, and Akshita; my friends: Ankit, Aryaman, Arnav, and Nadu; and my first teachers.

Life at the boarding school was filled with many experiences. At the top of my 'what have I gained' list is a sense of humour, a physically fit body (I am fabulously good-looking now), a better sense of style (because I was already good at it), the power of self-study (away from the world of tuition), better reading habits, and learning to be with other people and accepting them as they are.

Though I do miss the comfort of my bed, sleep, my phone, waffles, and ice cream, the challenges at the boarding school have been many! **Fake it till you make it** summarises how I learned to swim and how it helped me win at the district level and represent the state.

The challenge was that I was being delusional and overconfident when I joined swimming at school. Our school encouraged everyone to learn swimming not just because it was a sport but also because it was a life skill. My challenge—I THOUGHT I could swim. It was when I nearly drowned that I got a reality check. I was stubborn enough to continue to fake it until it became clear to the coach and all those who watched me that my belief that I could swim was not a reality. My first challenge was to accept it and the second was to try and learn to do it the right way. This pretence turned into actual learning because my coach didn't give up on me. This changed me from someone who could not breathe underwater to one who could do 32 laps every day as a casual warm-up and from someone who merely floated to one who competed to better her score from 1 minute to 53 seconds and then 51 seconds. I am now challenging myself to get better every day.

I realised the bigger challenge was to be consistently good and be determined to push myself every second, to accept what I didn't know and to learn to do it right.

Just then, I was faced with another challenge, to move from the **'Me to Us' mindset**. This was when I went on the Leadership Trek to Dharamshala. I realised that friendships can be worth a lot.

I am now going to tell you about the things my friends did for each other, the challenges we faced, and how that changed the way I look at friendships. The boys in my class, who my friends and I thought were weird, acted differently on this trek. I mean, they were not weird at all! They were helpful, caring, and serious for the first time. Was there something wrong with them? Was it the chill? Did they have a fever? I mean, we could not understand how they were so different from the 'I don't care' demeanour that we saw every day at school.

They helped by picking up heavy suitcases, lending their jackets when the temperature dropped, guiding us through the snow by telling us exactly where to step for safety, and lending us a helping hand to climb heights—what was happening? They had become a support group instead of chaos creators!

We were struggling to walk through the snowy patches and were unable to use the washroom. Our tents were leaking due to the heavy rain, and we suffered through cramps, pain, and even broken shoes. We managed to survive and get out of the snow mountains alive! Now when I look back, the worst situations brought out the best in all of us. I can now say that the trek was worth it!

I understood the meaning of how the 'I to Us' concept works. I experienced how people can actually change in seconds, from being self-centred to helping others and making things better for them. The trek taught me that people may appear hard or cold on the outside, but they might be the sweetest ones when you actually talk to them or get to know them. We learned to give and accept things from each other as well.

You don't always have to go on a trek; you may face challenges every day at a boarding school. I mean it. They can be beyond your imagination! Since I learned to deal with it, it did not register as a challenge in my mind's hard disk. Only the bigger challenges have earned their place in this book.

On that note, the biggest challenge I dealt with was feeling homesick! This symptom would occur twice or thrice a year and when it would happen, I would fall sick, get a fever and be visibly unwell. Things got so bad that I had to be immediately picked up and taken home, so my health would not deteriorate any further.

Now! Now! Now! I know what you're thinking.

"Cyra, didn't you tell us that you did not remember or miss home?"

My answer is still No! I did not miss home, but sometimes after seeing my friends and roommates miss home, I also started missing home a lot. Like, a LOT!

The immediate effect was I started overthinking a LOT. Because of overthinking, I would get sick, a LOT! Since this was not a normal thing, I would seek permission to call my parents and the 'a LOT' would make them pick me up the very next day! I would be home the next day.

Someone said, "Wow, Cyra! You get taken care of by your parents!"

Of course, they do! I am their only child. They are my strongest support system. Well, I do not mean to sound boring, but boarding school made me realise that my family is my 'life jacket.'

And sometimes, in my stormy hostel, there are episodes where I feel that my life jacket is missing! So, I run and grab it.

My parents are my rock. They are always standing beside me, without being fazed by anything. They fight for me, especially when anyone does something wrong to me. They are my biggest cheerleaders—thrilled about my wins, emotional to see me perform on stage, excited to see my sketch put up in an exhibition, cheering from the stands on sports days, and always taking pride in every single thing I do. Every single thing!

Sometimes, I have to tell them, "Dude! It's ok! It's normal."

I got my looks, style, and continuous talking mouth from my mother. I have known her for 15 years now and am happy to say she will never change. Her hobby is to become emotional, to hurry things up, and to annoy the hell out of me! But even then, she is very, very, actually super possessive about me.

How? You may ask!

OK, let me give you an example. I would get a small cut or whatever, and there she would be, crying her eyes out, calling the ambulance and I don't know what else. She cannot see me get hurt or be in pain. And another thing, if she makes up her mind or decides something, it's impossible to change it. Even God Himself won't be able to change her mind. And forget about winning an argument with her. It's impossible. So, if you ever get into a fight with her, give up your hopes of winning and accept defeat from the start. That's my mom!

I got my personality, the laugh and the 'I love annoying people a lot' streak from my father. His hobby is sending me random reels on Instagram, calling me randomly just to show me his face, and throwing pillows at me to annoy me. After all this, he cries in front of me whenever he feels emotional. How? Let me give you an example. I would be in my room when suddenly my dad would hug me, tears flowing from his eyes.

"Pa, are you OK?" I would ask.

My father would reply, while hugging me tightly "Cyra! I know that I'm the best person you have ever met and that you will not be able to live without me, so I'll shift in with you after your marriage. I am just telling you, that I love you too!" (even when I have not said I love you at that moment).

This happens more often than you think it does. Even after they act in such an annoying fashion, I still know that they will support me and cheer me on, through everything and anything that might come my way.

There are five girls in my room. When I cry for silly reasons, these roommates are always there for me. Even if it is midnight, they are always there to comfort me. My roommates have gone from being total strangers to good friends to best friends and now my family. I might not tell them that they are my best friends; I would usually say that they are my good friends, but I would never be able to deny my true feelings as I think of them as my best friends, my family (and room three). The truth is that they know me better than I even know myself.

My boarding school is a place where people willingly come to help you when you need something. There are motivators, there are people who discipline you, there are uplifters, and there are a zillion friends. Suddenly, someone would appear from somewhere, and you would get exactly what you need at that time.

My boarding school taught me a big rule of survival—**No one will know until you tell them!**

If I am sick, or I need something, or if I am undergoing a strong emotion, I have to tell others. No one can guess how I feel. As I say this, I must admit that our teachers could read us very well. They could tell if something was wrong from our body language and by how we greeted them and our expressions even if we didn't vocalise it. They would wait for us to open up, but if we didn't, there was always someone who would take us for a walk on the campus or talk to us in the cafeteria to help decode the emotional mystery in our heads. Because they were always watching and looking out for us.

In a boarding school, the teachers help you fight many fears. I could express the fear I experienced when I looked at numbers to my math teacher. He did not judge me at all. He taught me to fight my fear first. He made me look at every little progress positively. He held my hand through my most fearful moments and made me feel confident. My school taught me to express myself. To speak up. About myself. And for myself.

My inclination towards sports and my entire life at boarding school have shown me that I underestimate myself. However, I have learned that **"I am more strong, mentally and physically, than I think."**

This fact hit me hard when I participated in my first-ever triathlon. For those who don't know, I had to first swim, then cycle, and then race. Believe me, it is tougher than you can imagine. Whatever you have imagined just now, multiply it by the biggest number you know! When the triathlon was about to begin, I started questioning and doubting myself. I even doubted my life choices at that time!

"Why did I decide to do this?" And the next thought was, "Why did I decide to do this to myself?"

Please do not misunderstand—a triathlon is not just about three back-to-back races. NO! It tests your mental toughness before your physical endurance. I mean it! You have to endure intense physical pain, while your mind keeps pushing you to not give up. You may faint or fall, but you have to make it to the finish line. Guess what? That is a triathlon!

There was serious competition, and despite participating for the first time, I secured third place. The bronze medal was mine! It was only after I recovered from the cramps and pain that I realised I had more within me than I had thought!

I never judge people. Never.

People asked me about my experience of interacting with my schoolmates, especially because they were from different parts of the country. I must admit, that even though the names of their towns and cities improved my geography skills, the fact is that they were just like me and I was just like them. We were all the same. It didn't even matter to us. We were friends, roommates, classmates, and buddies, that's all. It was only a few words that they spoke differently. And, by the way, we made an effort to learn each other's language. How we thought, reacted, and dealt with life was just the same. We accepted how each one ate, spoke, behaved, and even reacted. **Boarding school taught me we were all the same**. We were tied by our friendship and not by where we lived or came from. We accepted each other as we were. We accepted each other's shortcomings and strengths, habits, and choices. We may have shouted, fought, appreciated, and even criticised each other in our rooms, but in the end, we accepted each other.

It is when you enter a boarding school that you realise that you are responsible for yourself. You cannot know that anywhere else at the age of 14. We learned, **"I am responsible for myself"**.

I am responsible for:

How I look
How I behave
How I talk and
What I choose
I get to decide how my story goes.

Similarly, you have better and worse examples all around you. You are always watching and you are responsible for what you choose. But with continued observation, I have realised that I am responsible for creating a better version of myself, not worse. I am proud that I have made the right choices.

Personally, while I choose to be responsible, I choose to have a better sense of humour as well!

Delulu is the only Solulu!

Humour saves your soul! That is the biggest truth! It is humour that saves you through this journey.

I have developed a great sense of humour, ever since I arrived at the boarding school. I can mimic things like I never could before. I can even tell what the other person would say. Living in a world of 'buffoons,' using 'aiyo' to express a variety of emotions like sadness, surprise or happiness, where people are tripping on oxygen around me! Remember, I told you I am mostly happy because I have found humour around me and in the way I deal with things! (and for the ones from 1500 BC who do not know the meaning of this header, it means 'being delusional is the only solution!')

It is a completely different life. You have to live it to understand it. There is no other way.

Either you are a boarding school kid or you are not.

No chapter can ever tell you all about a boarding school. It grows on you. And it helps you grow.

It becomes a part of your introduction. "I am a boarding school product," and that says it all.

Like I said in the beginning, I have taken a different road. I still remember a serious conversation that both my parents had with me, many times over, when we were getting ready to join the boarding school.

They told me, "Cyra, you will realise that children will come to your boarding school for different reasons. Always remember your reason. You are not going to the boarding school as a form of punishment or correction. You are going to the boarding school for developmental reasons only."

My mother always said, "Cyra, you can be so much more!" and that is what I went to the boarding school for. To see what more I could become and even try to become that.

I have fought many fears, experienced many new things, and become independent and responsible. I have learned to fight, to never give up, to still try.

I have understood the value of friendships and I have learned to give support and to share.

I have become determined.

I know one thing for sure, I am improving every day.

I am truly like the moon, imperfect yet beautiful. I still have some marks, but I have learned to embrace the beauty of how I truly am. The school made me realise that improving bit by bit every day is better than not making any progress at all.

I often hear this in school, "Do the best you can until you know better. Then when you know better, do better."

I have two more years left at that amazing place. A place that will always be responsible for shaping my thought process, personality, and the way I look at life. I am sure there are many more beautiful experiences and adventures awaiting me.

I know I miss my sleep and my home, but I know for sure that the day when this journey concludes and I step out into the outer world, I will miss this one.

I am still learning patiently, waiting for the day when I will successfully complete the chapter I have started. But for now, I look at the long path I still have to walk, with its ups and downs. I am ready to face it and become braver than I was.

In the words of Merida from the movie Brave,

"Some say fate is beyond our command.
But I know better.
Our destiny is within us.
You just have to be BRAVE enough to see it."

Cyra Arora is a 15-year-old with a great sense of humour. She loves art, sports, horror movies, reading, and staying happy. She obtained her life skills: independence and responsibility from the boarding school. Her resilience and persistence got her a place in the India Book of Records. She believes in the beauty of imperfection and often says, "Delulu is the only Solulu."

TRUE TALE 4

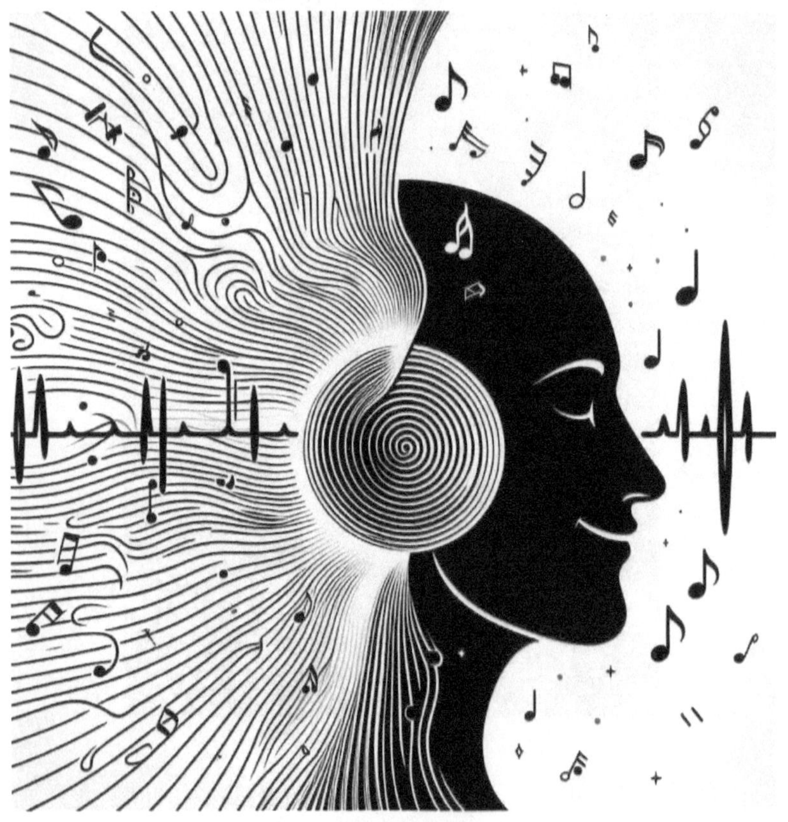

THE MELODIOUS JOURNEY OF MY RHYTHMIC HEARTBEAT

SYNA AGGARWAL

The Melodious Journey of My Rhythmic Heartbeat

Do you know this fact about bamboo trees?

A bamboo tree grows underground for a long time before it shoots up above the ground. It takes five years for a Chinese bamboo tree to break through the soil. Once it does, it will grow to a height of 90 feet in just five weeks!

Why did I begin the story of my journey with the analogy of a bamboo tree?

As they say, what looks like success is often just patience. To understand why I mentioned the bamboo tree and relate it to success and patience, let me take you back 10 years. Yes, a whole decade. Three words—stuffed toys, a pretend microphone, and an 8-year-old 'casual' bedroom singer. This is where my visualisation of 'I want to be a singer' started or rather when I sowed the seeds of the bamboo tree.

My fascination with things differed drastically from other kids of my age. While my friends played with Barbies and Hot Wheels, I went to the toy store and got myself a toy piano. Everything about instruments and music charged me with enthusiasm. Dressed in a frilly frock, I would sit and play the piano all day, even when I barely knew any notes. As an 8-year-old, I wasn't fully aware of my musical inclinations, but I remember feeling completely drawn to it. That, my friends, is where my mom proved to be a true blessing.

She entered my room one day while I was pretending to perform at a concert, as the best singer in the world! She silently observed, paused, and told me that my voice had something special, something unique in it, something that most pretend singers didn't have. At the time, I didn't think much of it. As a child, I assumed that my mom was just praising me. However, praises, if they are consistent and come from different people, do make you take notice. Soon, my family and friends began telling me that I sing well, and that's when I started realising that music and I shared a unique bond. My eyes started shining and I couldn't stop smiling.

That is true even now. Today, the moment I start singing, I am soaring high, almost straight to the sun in just a wink. One evening, during a family dinner, as usual, I sat in the living room with the toy piano. Mind you, it was barely a piano, but I played it with nothing short of Beethoven's zeal! I was singing a song that I had very recently grown fond of. At the same time, one of my parents' family friends entered the living room. Out of sheer nervousness, I stopped playing. I clearly remember what he told me then.

He said, "If you love it, don't let anyone's presence or anything stop you." That thought registered in my mind.

A question, however, still bothered me. How will I know if I love it? The realisation and the answer soon followed. I thought about the hours I had spent doing this, even as a child. Of course, as an 8-year-old, I simply saw it as something I enjoyed doing over and over again.

As I understand it now and can decode, music was forming connections for me and with me. I would get lost in it, feel absorbed, and at times even experience what seemed like a connection to a superpower. This transition from a spark to the sun, along with the joy, happiness, and fulfilment it brought, was something I began seeking more and more. As I grew older, I told my mom that music was more than just a pastime—it gave me a sense of joy and unimaginable happiness, and that I wanted to feel that more often, perhaps all the time. Then doing what mothers do, she put things into action. She enrolled me in classes, and I started exploring different genres.

But wait, I want you to know that I started my journey as a pianist. Singing along was something I did out of habit. It was at that moment that my mentor made me realise that my singing wasn't just habitual. I enjoyed it because I had a natural understanding of 'sur'. And right there, I took a break from my piano playing and started exploring the glorious field of vocals.

Though it took hours of practice every day, I embraced the challenge with enthusiasm. My mentor had a significant role in helping me flourish because he never gave me easy tasks. Even as a beginner, he made me learn the most complex songs, sometimes leaving me baffled. But I knew I had to push myself to turn my 'pretend' dream into reality. I started with Celine Dion, Mariah Carey, and Alicia Keys, and then slowly explored songs by Lata Mangeshkar, Alka Yagnik, and Asha Bhosle, which were more connected to our Indian traditional background.

He made sure that my roots as a singer were strong, just like the bamboo tree. He knew that once the roots were well-formed, the battle would be won. He was constantly making sure that my practice made me strong enough to never consider giving up. This is why I resonate completely with the bamboo tree. The bamboo is a symbol of longevity because of its durability, strength, flexibility, and resilience. It survives in the harshest conditions, standing tall and staying green year-round. This was exactly what I was doing! This was where I learned my very first lesson.

In fifth grade, I entered my first inter-school competition. Heart racing, hands cold, and with a certain shiver in my voice, I was a nervous wreck indeed. The practice for this went on for days—it was eight to nine hours of non-stop vocal practice every day. The desire was to feel that victorious rush on the first try. I entered the competition area and was completely shocked. All the other participants were much older than me! They had had at least seven years of practice, so they were clearly ahead of me.

A nervous thought struck me, "What should I do? Am I even good enough? Will I even stand a chance?"

I began to doubt myself—my voice hadn't even matured. What do I do now? A firm believer in Lord Hanuman, I started reciting the Hanuman Chalisa as a form of vocal warm-up. Faith can do wonders! As I continued to recite it, my belief in Him started calming my nerves one by one, so deeply that I continued to recite it.

Soon it was time. I went onstage, gave it my best shot, and with a strange nervousness, sat down to wait for the results. *Third place: XYZ person—gone. Second place: ABC person—gone.*

Talking to myself, I said, "I can't possibly get first. I have lost it. I'm not good enough."

But my faith and the inner child within me convinced me to continue humming the Hanuman Chalisa. Not just as a vocal warm-up, but for a sense of calmness because that's what my love for music and belief in Hanuman Ji had created.

And then, the moment came! *First place: Put your hands together for this one: Syna Aggarwal!*

"What just happened?" I thought. "What did I just hear?"

I couldn't believe it; I thought I was dreaming. I told my friends to pinch me as hard as they could but it turned out to be true. I was not an athlete, but the way I ran to grab that first-prize trophy, I was pretty sure I could give any sprinter a run for their money.

Going back to my analogy, perhaps a tiny green leaf of the bamboo tree was visible now. Perhaps the five-year journey of watering the bamboo tree was nearly over. That win marked a series of victories and achievements.

My mom got a call on a random day from our city's radio station, 92.7 BigFM, and guess who got called to sing there? As a child, I was undoubtedly confident. However, huge opportunities like these gave me jitters and a frightened feeling of 'Will I be good enough?'

With that aura of trepidation, I stepped inside and sang a song as a trial. I'm not going to lie, the first few lines of my 'trial song' were full of shivers and errors, and I knew it. It was as if my music was putting me through some test. But ultimately, there is no best friend with whom you don't have a little misunderstanding.

My self-belief took over. My passion pushed me and something inside me said, "This is something you love, Syna!"

I was reminded of anything and everything that I had been attempting within my power to be better each day. I decided that I would not let fear slap me in the face. Not when it was one of the biggest opportunities of my life, and the chance to make my best friend proud.

The same radio station later held a competition to find the 'Voice of the City.' My dad had always encouraged me and never missed an opportunity to boost my confidence with his presence. Be it a skating competition, or a music or dance performance, I had always taken him with me, and he just sat there, smiling as much as he could to give me that confidence. I didn't win the competition, but I did become the runner-up, earning the title of the 'Voice of the City' among participants that even included college students.

My dad hugged me with pride and affectionately said, "Synu, you did it!" A small child's voice beat the college students' voices: "Synu, your hard work paid off!"

Dad often said he didn't know how many prizes I would win, but he was certain that I was meant to do big things in life, leave a mark, and get noticed for my talents! That was when I realised that my friendship with music would open a thousand doors of opportunity for me. Music and I had built an inseparable bond that grew stronger minute by minute and day after day. But with this connection came the inevitable challenges, hardships, and hurdles.

Then came the time for my second inter-school competition. Till then, I had participated quite a lot. With the same confidence and belief that my voice and my music are my best friends always and forever, I went onstage. I never gave up on my hard work.

This time, it took about nine hours of practice every day for a week, and I was singing one of the best but most complex songs of Mariah Carey. I thought I would intimidate my competitors with my performance!

But that was when my overconfidence came back to bite me. I went onstage, thinking everything was perfect, but it wasn't. The sound of the piano was so loud that it overpowered my vocals. My voice couldn't return to its normal range, and the judges couldn't even hear me properly. I had no idea what was going on because my mic was such that all I could hear was me. Yet again, I sat in the chair, waiting for the results. This time my excitement was mixed with uncertainty. The third prize went to XYZ, the second prize to me and the first prize to ABC. I had been consistently getting first prizes and this was something new for me. I sat there in disbelief. This time, my 'getting the certificate walk' was slower than a snail's pace. I was disappointed in myself. As I fought back tears, I put on a smile just for the picture with the judges and then walked outside with my head down.

Once again, my heart was racing, and my hands and feet were cold, but this time, not from nervous excitement but from a deep disappointment. Was it that my music couldn't make me the best? Had I done something wrong and let it down? Had I disappointed my friend forever? My self-belief was shaken. The challenges did not stop there. Difficult scenarios kept coming, one after the other. They almost seemed unstoppable.

Well, so did the opportunities! I was invited to participate in various reality TV shows. It was one of my fantasies as a kid. I went to many of them, just trying to make my way through.

However, since I had just gotten the bitter taste of hardship, I was very sceptical about my musical 'talent.' Before reaching the final stage where a performer is supposed to sing in front of the judges on TV, everyone had to clear two to three rounds based in various cities. I went to the first city and went inside the room. But this time, there was no excitement, just fear—the fear of rejection, the fear of not doing well, the fear of failing music. And yet again, it happened. For a few more months, I kept getting invites from reality TV shows. I went, faced rejection in the first round itself and came back with glistening, teary eyes. In one of the auditions, I got through the first two rounds. Then I had my interview, the last stage before entering the stage. But unfortunately, it seemed as if my voice had slipped away from me, again. And yet again, my 12-year-old self came out crying.

It is said, "Disappointment is a temporary detour on the road to success."

My parents played a vital role in shaping me and teaching me how to handle disappointments and failures. The first thing my mom did was hold my hand in the car while we were coming back. She asked me a perspective-altering question, about whether I sang to hear 'Syna Aggarwal won' or did I sing to feel the joy, the thrill of learning something new, and the feeling of accomplishment that I got when I mastered a new skill in a new genre, or perhaps the feeling of being loved by melodies and rhythms, and the sweetness of my voice?

She introduced me to the connection I had with my rhythmic heartbeat. I understood how integral it was for me to sing for this bond, the one I shared with my voice and my music. The bond that had led me on this journey and was melodiously governed by my 'rhythmic heartbeat.'

That was a turning point for me, my perspective had altered. I just changed the way I viewed my results. I changed the way I looked at my accomplishments or even defeats. My mother got me a photo frame that said 'Mistakes are proof that you are trying,' and I was trying. That was when I realised that neither was music failing me nor was I failing music.

Every journey should be considered like a perfect cake with cherries on the top—a smooth surface with cherries (hurdles) in between.

The fact remains that my parents were never the type to give me false hopes. They always kept me grounded and connected with reality. There was bluntness, honesty, and authenticity in their feedback. As a kid, I felt like they were not appreciative of my singing. It turned out, that was what helped me become a better version of myself every day. Had I not received that constructive criticism, I would not have reached even the third round of auditions. I would not have won the first prize in my first inter-school competition as a fifth-grader against twelfth-graders, and I would not have thought that music was something that gave me innate happiness, regardless of the achievements.

I started working even harder, and just like the bamboo tree, my roots became stronger too. I got ready to face anything and everything. I learned to find joy in the smallest of achievements. This sense of realisation grew stronger when the COVID-19 pandemic hit. I had changed schools in grade seven. In grade eight, before I could make strong friendships, a worldwide lockdown was established. I lost contact with my previous school, and I had not yet made strong friendships in my new school. There came yet another wave of anxiety, palpitations, overthinking, random anxiety attacks, and constant self-nagging. I was free the whole day and I had time to think about unnecessary things the entire day. I thought about things like what is my worth. My mom calmed me down and asked me to think about what I really loved. And my answer was my music, my only possible friend at that time.

Now what could I do to distract myself?

I had a piano and a guitar. But I didn't know how to play the guitar. And right then, I went on YouTube and invested the entire day in learning how to play the guitar, all by myself. I practised till my fingers were sore with cuts. But that hard work, even though it did not make me the perfect guitarist, added to the list of instruments I could play. Now there was an addition to my musical rollercoaster, and I had done it all by myself, without any help. That was what made me come back to the normal jovial person that I was. My self-belief was soaring high! Music again proved to be the perfect remedy for my mental well-being. Now I knew that my love for music was not just one-sided. Music loved me too, so much that it could heal me. What a superpower! Did you know that music therapy is the most studied of all art therapies? Some components of music therapy include active listening, improvisational music playing, songwriting, and the meaning of lyrics. No wonder I was already better!

Well, one road led to the other! Another opportunity came my way. In grade eight, I had to represent my school in an all-India inter-school semi-classical singing competition. Semi-classical was something that I had never ever explored. How much time did I have? Five days. And mind you, my birthday was in between.

My first reaction was to my parents. "I don't think I can do it, mom and dad. It's semi-classical; I'm more of a Western vocalist. What should I do? Should I let this opportunity slip away?"

Even though that seemed like the easy way out, my parents told me one thing. They said, "Synu, just give it your best shot like you always have. Don't let the fear of not being good get to you, because as long as you work for it, you have already achieved that level of perfection in our eyes." This line too, like so many of their pieces of advice, stuck with me.

I did it. I practised for hours daily to learn the most complex works of Lata Mangeshkar. It was certainly a challenge. I did not know how to master those vocal modulations so well, and Lata Mangeshkar herself was an icon. Mind you, it was an online competition, so the fear of 'what if I start singing well and my net gives up' was a very big addition to my cold feet. But yet again, I hummed the Hanuman Chalisa and did it. There were around fifty schools from all over India in that competition, and I still managed to get the third position. I was on cloud nine. Had my voice just given me a tight hug when I worked to learn something new? Yes. I had made music proud, again.

Slowly and gradually, like the bamboo tree, I had begun to appear. I had come out of the ground, still small, but my roots were stronger than ever. I was taking my own sweet time to grow, and I still am. But I know very well that one day, I will reach the sky and become as tall as the bamboo tree.

After that, there was no stopping me. Now that I had started finding happiness even with participation alone, I seized every opportunity that I got. I shifted schools again in grade 11, but this time I went to a boarding school, away from home. However, I found friends there that turned into family a bit too quickly, and they were my sounding board. They were the ones who told me if there was something I could improve with my music and who cheered the loudest when I sang well. Music soon became my identity.

I have performed so much at the school that even if I hadn't talked to someone, they would say, "Oh, you're the one who sings, right?" and that would make my heart swell with immense glee.

We had many projects to add to our social service, including tutoring at a centre called Snehagram, which is a centre for HIV-positive children, and at an orphanage called Thayi Mane. Both these places were not just tutoring for me. I seemed to connect with the kids on a deeper level, and at both places, I either sang for or with the kids. At the orphanage, there were kids half my age who had the biggest smiles on their faces, even considering the situation they were in. That is when I thought that this was not just a school project for me. One of those kids was a music enthusiast. She could sing well, and at the end of my teaching hour, I went outside where all my friends were playing with the other kids. I sat on the floor with that little innocent girl, singing as many songs as she wanted to.

I was impressed by her zeal to learn more about music, and it made me smile unstoppably when she said, "Akka, you sing so well, akka. I love singing with you, it makes me feel so special, akka."

That statement brought happy tears to my eyes, and I felt like I was making a difference in somebody's life with the help of my music. I started resonating with her, the way music made me feel special. With the help of my best friend (my voice), I was making that little innocent girl feel better.

In the end, when we were all supposed to leave, she asked, "Akka, next time when you come, will you sing with me again?" and I replied, "It would be my greatest pleasure, sweetheart," and I hugged her and went back to school.

Time passed swiftly and I got another opportunity. I had the chance to be part of a music seminar that I co-conducted with one of my peers from the boarding school. The seminar was for a non-profit organisation (NPO) which provided shelter and educational opportunities for children from socially and economically disadvantaged backgrounds who were eager to learn. When I entered, I saw their faces. They were all giggly and excited about the seminar and that is when I thought to myself that I wanted them to know that if I could do it, they could too. I sang for about an hour after which I proceeded to sit down on the floor with them and sing. The comments that the kids were passing made me happier minute by minute. There was a girl by my side, whose friends said that she loved to sing. I, with the zeal to motivate and make a change, asked her to sing with me.

We sang for a long time, after which I asked her, "Who is your favourite singer?" That little girl replied, "Akka, you are my favourite singer. Akka, if I become like you when I grow up, I will be more than happy."

Yet again, I had tears in my eyes, and I knew that my hard work had paid off the moment I became an idol for young children. You did it, voice. We did it.

I got another chance to shine when I got an opportunity to be part of a gig at a café in Bangalore, my first ticketed event. I was a part of the school jazz band, and this was a new genre for me to explore. Again, silly old me, I took on the works of Frank Sinatra and Ella, the greatest jazz icons ever. My dad flew to Bangalore just to see my performance, and that, as always, was a confidence booster.

Not just through achievements, my music helped me express my emotions towards people who mean the world to me. I was really close to my great-grandma, and lovingly called her 'badi daadi.' My memories were of always going into her room and asking for biscuits that she kept just for us, her great-grandkids. One morning, I got to know that she was no more. It was a devastating moment, and all I could think of were my little moments with her and the innumerable memories that I had formed with her. Her smile continued to reflect in my mind, and there was a bright ray of light which surrounded her warm self. Here too, I expressed my deep connection with her by singing the prayers at her death ceremony. Music had always helped me make connections, and this was my way of reaching out to her through God, a way of telling her how much I loved her, and how I would always feel so. I put all my heart into preparing for this, and even though there was only one day left for her death ceremony, I put the whole day into it. I cannot recall even having food that day. All I remember is doing it just for her, to make sure she knew that her memories would never fade from her Synu's mind. And that is how I, with the help of music, could reconnect to 'badi daadi' again, and tell her for the last time, that she would always be with me, in my heart and my mind.

Now, the bamboo tree has grown taller, with roots strengthened by experience. The spark inside me has transformed into something much bigger. Throughout this journey, I've learned a great deal, not only about my music but also about life itself.

I understand several things now. Firstly, hard work is the most important factor. By this I mean don't follow the famous phrase of 'work smarter, not harder' because the people who work harder and not smarter are the ones who taste success for a longer period of time. That is what differentiated Lata Mangeshkar from any other singer who found shortcuts to success. If you are given everything on a plate, then that is not your success in the first place, that is the success of the person who prepared that well-garnished plate for you. So, if you want to reach success, pave your own way and make it your own success. Taste the bitterness of difficulties and the sweetness of achievements but pave it brick by brick, yourself. That is what makes success seem so flowery and beautiful because you realise that it was all you. I put in hours of practice every day, and I still am not perfect. However, the improvement has been humongous.

This brings me to the second lesson I learned. The English teacher at my previous school always used to tell me 'There is always room for improvement,' and that is indeed very true.

Even though you might feel like you have mastered something, you may not be perfect. However, that is what adds to the sweetness of any journey.

Thirdly, your sounding board is very important. This may vary from person to person; some people may feel like praise leads to motivation and better performance. However, my perception says that if you are not being criticised at every step, or if you are not being given truthful feedback, then you cannot improve further. For me, both of my parents had crystal clear opinions on where I had gone wrong, and that is how I strove to become better every day.

If not for them, I would not have reached where I am today; I would have still been the pretend vocalist in my bedroom. Be mindful of the people you take feedback from because they can either make your performance 'the ultimate one' or break it.

Lastly, true richness lies in knowing that you can never be the best. There is always someone better than you, and therefore having a humble personality, even when you have mastered your passion, is a necessity. Nobody likes to idolise or even talk to a very talented person who exudes arrogance. In a world full of unfairness and inhumanity, be the person who does not confuse profession with ego. That is what allows you to shine in a room where there may be no light. In a forest full of tall dark trees, become that one white flower, the prettiest among the lot but still the sweetest. Remember, if the Almighty can hold your hand till you reach success, He can also leave it the moment you start slipping away from being the humble person that you were as a beginner. There is something known as karma, and it exists for sure. So, no matter how much money you earn, be selfless, because royalty and richness are not defined by your net worth or the money you have, but they lie in your heart and the personality you portray.

The Chinese bamboo tree is a perfect parable about my own experience with personal growth and change. It's never easy, progress is often slow, and frustrating and unrewarding at times. But it is worth it, especially if we remain patient and persistent.

And this, my friends, was my melodious journey.

The bamboo tree is still growing, its roots are becoming deeper and stronger every day. With just the right care and a bit more time, it will be on its way to reaching the sky. I too am trying to reach a stage of professionalism, and all that I need now is my best friend, my voice, and my music to be there with me every single day. I also promise to give it my sweat, dedication, and honest practice.

Music has helped me answer some integral questions:

Can we stay focused and continue to believe in what we are doing even when we don't see immediate results? Music taught me that yes, we can.

In a culture driven by intense gratification, can we believe in the process? Yes, we can.

Can we follow the path of our rhythmic heartbeats and walk this melodious journey just for the connection and for the sheer joy it brings? Yes! We can.

My melodious journey thus far has taught me that the true beauty of music is that it connects people and hearts. Where words fail, music speaks. I am all set to listen to the language of music, to learn, play, and sing! I have not even begun; I have the whole world to explore and a hundred thousand things to learn. I am sure there are many of you like me who are trying to succeed with a passion. Let us have faith in the process, let us continue to walk even when we fall, and let us continue making connections.

For me, it started with Mariah Carey, and so I kept reading what she said at Madison Square Garden in 1995. She said, "This is for all of you out there tonight, reaching for a dream—don't ever give up!"

I promise I won't!

Syna Aggarwal is an 18-year-old passionate singer who wears her heart on her sleeve. Music is her sanctuary. When she's not singing, you can find her lost in her thoughts, daydreaming about life, love, and everything in between. She believes in being true to herself and following her heart.

TRUE TALE 5

THE FIRST STROKE OF MY MAGNUM OPUS

MANICKA KUMAR

The First Stroke of My Magnum Opus

Have you ever sat in a quiet room and closed your eyes as the clock faintly ticks in the background and all your thoughts fell apart to the utter silence in your brain? In those moments, what do you see? I see the mountains, rivers, and cool breeze as the iridescent moonlight falls on my skin while the stars dance in the night sky. I see myself in the middle of a valley with white flowers all around me but not in a way that most people do. I see it in a way that only I can understand. I see it in the most romanticised way when I am 'incandescently' happy with myself, like in a Jane Austen novel.

In those moments, I imagine how the sun, the brightest star in the sky, shines with unmatched brilliance, while the moon, merely a natural satellite without its own light, reflects the sun's radiance. Yet, it is the moon that inspires poetry, becomes the ultimate symbol of beauty, and is celebrated despite its imperfections.

I think again and wonder, "Am I just romanticising the moon or is it, in fact, true that the most beautiful things are perfectly attuned?"

I think that while romanticising things; you delude yourself into believing that the best things are found when you are happy or when everything around you is perfect.

Sometimes, I wonder what 'incandescent happiness' truly means, and that's why I want to share my story with you. This story isn't just about happiness but about the journey one undertakes to find joy in every fleeting moment rather than searching for moments that bring joy. It's a tale of sadness, self-doubt, and the hardships that ordinary people endure in their ordinary lives—without trivialising the weight of their seemingly small struggles. It's an ode to the idea that, no matter how dark the path may seem, you will emerge happier on the other side.

My story is an honest attempt to reassure you that there's a spark within each of us, and every struggle we endure, every path we tread, is part of a greater design meant to teach us the lessons we need to fulfil our purpose. The truth is, the universe is working for you, not against you. You may not see it now, but soon, a time will come when you'll realise that every piece of the puzzle fits perfectly.

Rumi once said, "The wound is the place where the light enters you," and this holds true for every struggle, every moment of pain, and every piece of our life's puzzle. It is all a part of a greater purpose, guiding us towards fulfilment and clarity.

Let's start from the incomplete puzzle I shared earlier and add a few more pieces to it: A 5'9" girl with long, straight, slightly layered hair is sitting on a log near the riverbed. She wears a stunning wine-coloured gown. It is body-fitting with a long trailing hem and a touch of a backless design. Her oval-shaped face is framed by bushy eyebrows, almond eyes, and a sharp nose with fine lips. Her physique is somewhere between an hourglass and a pear shape. If you haven't already guessed, that's me. And if you haven't figured out from how I describe myself, let me clarify—I'm quite self-absorbed, with an incredibly high opinion of myself, so please bear with me as I tell you about the many things I am.

I'll begin by telling you about the most constant thing in my life till now—acting. I was two years old when I played my first role as a mom in my school play and ever since then, I've participated in various plays. At the centre of the stage, with the spotlight on me, and me at my expressive best—this is where my self-absorbed nature stems from. As actors, we must possess such a high level of self-esteem that we must somehow manage to persuade the audience to believe our character's likes, truths, pains, joys and umpteen other emotions are our own. It wasn't long before my passion had multiplied manifold and at four years old, I was playing the main character in the annual day of my school which was more than satisfactory to my younger self.

The performing arts grew on me from an early age. By the time I was six, I was taking singing classes. I vividly remember my father staying up with me until midnight to help me prepare for a singing competition the next day. I sang *Let It Go* from *Frozen*. It was all that the younger version of me wanted to sing and I managed to secure second place. I was proud, but my father was even prouder. He has always been an enthusiast when it comes to the performing arts. He still reminds me that he used to direct all his school plays himself. Not only that, he also used to act in them.

Another thing that impacted my love for the performing arts was our relocation to Mumbai for six years. I branched out further with my parents enrolling me in art classes, dance classes, music classes, etc. I was 10 years old when we shifted back to Gurugram and there, my mother enrolled me in Kathak classes, and I delivered some very graceful performances. Soon enough, I also learned charcoal painting and made some very interesting pieces.

Before you jump to conclusions, thinking this girl who loves performance art must be pursuing something creative, let me clarify. I've chosen engineering! Surprised? I hope this doesn't cast any doubts on the piece of the puzzle you've just picked up. Yes, engineering!

This is also the perfect time to mention that my creative side is matched by my academic aptitude. Last year, in the tenth grade, I scored 55/56 in the IB MYP (International Baccalaureate Middle Years Programme). While it was not a flawless 56/56 like some of my classmates, I believe life is about balance—after all, you can't have it all!

The truth is, I am an eclectic person, and that defines me. Whether I'm dancing, singing, acting, playing, or writing, I feel truly content. This multifaceted side of me is paired with another defining trait—I am a thinker.

I reflect deeply on myself, others, and the world. I think about what I should and, at times, about what I shouldn't do. It's a constant stream of thought that can occasionally feel overwhelming or strange, but it's an intrinsic part of who I am.

But yes, the story must be worth a read, otherwise, what's the point? And that brings me to the point that no matter how eclectic I may be, I have lived the most ordinary life a 16-year-old can. However, what made me write this chapter is the twist that turned this 'ordinary' life into an 'extraordinary' example of grit, resilience, self-belief, and abundant courage. The past year and a half of my life will highlight how I dealt with my struggles to prioritise and even internalise my peace of mind and happiness. So let the story begin!

I remember the second day of tenth grade distinctly because it was the key moment in my life when I realised that my emotions were a lot more complex than I ever thought. I was sitting in the school counsellor's office, with her sitting across the table and me looking at her with tearful eyes. I was crying relentlessly with deep sobs with absolutely no clue of why I couldn't stop. There was a large window pane five metres on my left with the sun's rays peeking at me, and I remember faintly looking at the sun and just sobbing.

The counsellor held my hand and said, "I am here with you," but I looked down at our hands and thought, "Why is it that everybody is around me and yet I don't feel the same sense of belonging?"

She kept asking me, and I couldn't explain, but for a second, for the sake of not annoying her, I finally broke my silence and muttered, "I feel so lonely."

'Lonely,' what a simple word it was! Was I lonely because I didn't have friends? Or was it because the teachers didn't like me? Or because my parents never cared enough about my life? These are the most basic assumptions anybody would make if a 15-year-old came up to you and told you that she is lonely.

As I kept crying, she looked me in the eye and told me that I was in a class that had board exams and that maybe I was just stressed about the pressure that came with scoring well.

She even asked me, "What is your period date?"

I looked at her and for a second I wanted to laugh because why did it feel like she was just finding a reason for my grief when I couldn't care less about it? The only thing that I wanted was to stop feeling this way. Yes, I was feeling what I was feeling and there was no definite reason for it. I was just feeling it. All I knew for sure was that it wasn't because of my period.

I think there comes a time when you long for the presence of your people—not just living, breathing individuals, but those who truly make you feel at home. I've always struggled to understand who my people are and who genuinely deserve to matter in my life. During this particular period, I was running low on my 'friend count.' With fewer friends around, I began to see how unkind people could be. One girl in my class stood out in this regard. While we weren't exactly friends, we often spoke to one another. She had a reputation for being arrogant, making fun of others, and believing that she was superior. Her targets were not limited to classmates; sometimes, she directed her mockery even at our teachers.

The reason she gets to be a part of my story is that her scarily high level of insensitivity made me realise that I was surrounded by many like her. The lack of empathy and the shared sense of community became so evident that I too found myself guilty of being insensitive to somebody, just like her and the others.

A lack of connection with my insensitive, criticising self, pushed me to a stage of disbelief in myself. So much so that it was uncontrollably shattering. Shattering enough to wake me to a moment of realisation that losing my warmth, kindness, and compassion was a choice I did not want to make any longer. This stance that I took about maintaining my grace had multiple fallouts and impacts. The loss of friends was one. I started to think of it as a problem and somehow, I kept pointing the finger at myself as the cause of the problem. This stance and its corresponding actions would perturb me because socially, I was still trying to be cordial. However, nothing seemed to fall into place. Very soon I realised, I had no one around. Despite taking the right stance, which I reconfirm now, I was the one who was alienated. It was a dark place. I was feeling lonely, doubtful, questionable, insecure, unassertive and somewhat timid.

An equally big concern was the inability to communicate my emotions, the havoc they were creating, and all that I was experiencing. It had become so evident that I was in a state of breakdown, that my parents were summoned to come to the school to handle this worrisome situation. I was unable to communicate and was uncontrollably inconsolable.

I was sitting in the principal's office with my back to the door, facing her. The moment my father entered the room, I broke down again. I hugged him and kept crying.

I wanted to tell him, "Take me away, Papa, I want to go back to being your little girl."

I often imagine a world with two types of children—one where you grow and experience all the phases of life and another where God grants you the gift of staying a child forever. Let the soul choose for itself whether it truly wishes to grow up or remain in the innocence and wonder of childhood. If you ask me, I know my soul would choose to be a child forever.

On our drive back home, I made a few attempts to tell him what was going on inside me through broken expressions. His words, "I hear you," calmed me down.

He then stopped the car right outside our condominium to have a father-daughter conversation. After he had patiently heard my emotional gibberish, he said something that brought clarity to my perception.

I clearly remember each word he said. "I understand you. I clearly do. I can see why you are feeling lonely. It is at this junction of life, Manicka, that you need to understand that we can let other people impact us only to a point. People will come, but whether we let them stay on is our choice. They cannot stay to impact you negatively. Manicka, you know who you are. Be absolutely clear of your many strengths and most importantly what should matter to you. Do take all the emotional space you need to recover but remember your mind must clearly focus on what truly matters. Be clear about the people who must stay in your life and hence whether their departure from your life should matter to you. Some things are better lost, especially if they aren't making you better."

Yet again, my father stood like a rock beside me. In that silence, I was reminded of my journey as a debater. I hardly ever lost a debate, and if I did, I would call up my father and cry. My rock of Gibraltar would motivate me, and voilà, I would win all the subsequent debates. He got me. He understood my need to be the best at whatever I did. My career was as important as my intellectual, emotional, and social growth. On the days when I would not be the best at my studies, I would always picture myself on the top floor of a high rise in New York City facing the legendary skyline. That was my high moment and a liberating dream I shared with my father.

My father pointed towards a tall commercial building a little down the road with a multi-billion-dollar company's name on it. It was the tallest building around and the blue glass was beautifully reflecting the sun's rays.

He said, "Look at that building. See how it stands out, tall and bold. Just like you, Manicka," and continued, "When you sit in such a tall building and accomplish your dreams, you will have succeeded in life. At that moment, what people would have said or done wouldn't matter. It won't even matter if you feel lonely. What would truly matter would be the stance you took during the hard times. How you worked hard towards your goal and your success and, most importantly, the people you took along."

As they say, "Stay focused, go after your dreams and keep moving towards your goals."

When my father told me to go ahead and take my emotional space, he also knew that I would need to focus my energies constructively towards my goal, despite the emotional and social struggles. I set my eyes on the 10th-grade board preparations with diligence.

One line that stayed with me during this period was, "The future depends on what you do today."

I was not prepared to let it all go because I was hit by this storm that had shaken my self-belief. With repeated self-talk, affirmations, contemplation, and immense support from my parents, I chose to deal with it and also focus on the goal ahead of me. It was like walking with a heavy bag on my shoulder. I could balance it, change sides, hold it differently, but had to keep walking forward.

From the time I started this walk, I became more open to new people entering my life. I also became brave. I became comfortable being on my own and shielding myself from negativity and insensitivity. Though the heavy bag of sadness and depression still hung on my shoulder, I walked with my CHIN UP! This little attempt positively impacted the graph of my life. It was like an upward-opening parabola, and while I had fallen down the steep hill, I was still just hovering around the vertex somewhere at the bottom, attempting to climb back up.

Well, you can't win it all. My personality lost its shine along the way, and I realised that only two people, other than my family, really noticed that. The first one was my math teacher who came and sat with me during breakfast and asked me if I was going through something. The second was a girl who I had a beef with and I remembered from our annual camps.

I was sitting with her and she asked me, "Manicka, you've changed. It's like your spark is gone."

I looked at her, ready to defend myself, but I realised she was not wrong. It's funny how the people who you least expect to know you read you so well sometimes. With constant attempts to keep myself open and receptive, I had new friends come along. Some old friends came back too and a new grid was formed.

In the midst of all this, I made a crucial decision that would shape my college journey. Should I stick with IBDP (International

Baccalaureate Diploma Programme) or switch to CBSE (Central Board of Secondary Education)?

Engineering was my goal, but IB's high costs and its alignment with studying abroad posed challenges for my middle-class family. Scholarships seemed to be my only option for international universities like MIT (Massachusetts Institute of Technology). It was my dream school but it had its hauntingly low acceptance rates. Realising the risks, I chose CBSE, focusing on IIT (Indian Institute of Technology) while keeping my international options open. With my continuing struggles, I wasn't confident about myself, getting scholarships, or a high score in grade 10. With contemplation and discussions, the decision was made. I joined a CBSE school.

Soon after completing my last exam, I joined the new school. The first day was welcoming and warm, barring the fact that students from other sections came to have a 'look' at me! It was daunting. With the prominent feeling of being an outsider, I reached home and cried. Even though I had walked many miles now, I was still carrying the bag on my shoulder.

Despite a completely different atmosphere, being stuck in the same room from 0800 to 1400 hours, not moving around at all and making braids, I was trying my best to make space for myself. What concerned me the most was freedom of speech. Students could not speak freely. In fact, it was difficult to express one's opinion. This was contrary to my beliefs and the opposite of the culture of my earlier school.

A few days after joining the school, I auditioned for the theatre club. I thought this would be the way to claim my shine back!

The teacher-in-charge and the president of the club were sitting in the audience along with another girl who wanted to audition. They asked me to perform various scenes with different emotions, and as I performed, I could see their looks of amazement. It felt oddly satisfying because, on the one hand, this was something I had been doing all my life, and on the other, it had been so long since I met people who were rather amazed at this skill. When the audition was done, I went back to my classroom. A little while later, the president of the club called me and congratulated me for being chosen.

He said, "Not only have you been chosen but you have also been appointed as the general secretary of this club."

Another thing about me is that I do not react very drastically to surprises, so while I was surprised, I just said, "Thank you" and moved on. I felt a sense of satisfaction in being recognised for something that I had always loved. I saw a spark of my former shine!

A few days later, I learned about a major event happening at my school—a play based on the life of Rani Lakshmibai. I approached the teacher-in-charge and expressed my interest in auditioning. Having always played the lead role in previous plays, I naturally aimed for the main character. He called me to his class later that day and asked me to perform a few lines. I gave it my best shot or so I thought. A few hours later, I learned that another girl, one that the teacher had previously worked with, was chosen to play the lead.

I was incredibly disappointed when I was told that the reason for rejection had something to do with my British accent when I spoke Hindi. Honestly, while I do have a slight accent when

I speak English, I knew for sure that my Hindi was free of any such influence. Well, the teacher later called me for the role of the narrator. Since I had not done anything more than an audition to prove myself, I thought I'd take whatever I got. The narrator's lines were huge and, as any other actor would, I took my job very seriously even though it was a small part.

The practice sessions were fun. New friends, socialising and much laughter! However, in one interaction, I was judged again! During a discussion about a scene, someone asked me for my input.

Suddenly someone else said, "Well, she cannot act!"

I realised that being rejected for the main role had made an impression in people's minds. I had the urge to tell them that I had been acting since I was a little girl, but I could not. I don't blame them either because they had never seen me act.

In early August, my 10th-grade results were announced. They were initially set to be declared around 1730 hours, but there was a delay, and since my tuition was scheduled for 1800 hours, I had to leave before finding out. I won't lie. I wasn't expecting much, but I knew my parents were. As I sat in the auto on the way to my tuition with the cool breeze against my face, I listened to the emotional song 'Kun Faya Kun.' And I found myself praying to God. I had always been a topper, and I hoped this time wouldn't be any different. All my friends, except me, had received their results. I was on the verge of tears, but I walked into my tuition class and buried myself in my studies.

Suddenly, around 1824 hours, I received a call from my mom, and I could hear her screaming with excitement. She told me that I had scored 55/56 and that she was incredibly proud of me. I cried a little because, as shocked as I was, it made me realise how much I had underestimated myself. This was the first time in months that I truly saw how much I had doubted my potential. I had convinced myself that I would not be able to get into an international university with a scholarship. But the truth was, I had already proven I was capable of it. I had done well in the IB MYP. If I had believed in myself, then I might have achieved even more, like pursuing the IB DP and earning a scholarship to an international university.

Then came the day of the final show of the play on Rani Lakshmibai. The moment the final run started, I felt like I had fallen from grace because I watched the girl who played Manikarnika, and I must admit, she was phenomenal. The audience cried in the last scene. She was fighting an army of people alone, and she did not stop fighting till her last breath. And there I was, coming in between, when the scenes were switched in the dark, and reciting my pre-recorded lines. I didn't even have the spotlight on me. That day, I learned the grace of hugging and congratulating someone else and accepting that they had done a fantastic job, even though I was rejected for the same role.

I was known as the new girl in the grade, and there wasn't much else to my identity, except that I had a certain 'pretty privilege' because I fit conventional standards of beauty. I wasn't considered smart in this school because there were people in my class who were working incredibly hard towards cracking the JEE (Joint Entrance Examination). After all, that was their goal. I had become even more laid back because even though that's what I thought I wanted to do too; I don't think I was ever fully convinced by it.

The most important thing I learned there was inclusion because even though all these people were very different, they spoke to everyone. I learned that it's not too hard to go up to another person and ask them about their day. It may sound like a simple task as you read it, but in reality, it felt difficult and surprisingly easy at the same time. I was observing, absorbing, and learning from what I saw around me.

The school council had planned a week-long inter-house cultural and sports event. One of them was a theatre competition. I knew I had to participate. I somehow managed to send in an audition clip and was selected. One day before the final round, I was informed about my selection. I was a bit annoyed because I had to put together an act overnight, but that wasn't the time for excuses. I spent all night ideating a moving monologue based on the Kolkata rape case. I was playing the role of the victim and I was going to deliver a couple of lines on her feelings after she reached heaven.

I made some great props and decided on my costume, hair and makeup. The next day, I decided to go up on stage and deliver the monologue impromptu. Whenever I go up on stage, a wave of adrenaline takes over, so I do not remember much about the performance itself. What I did remember, however, was that by the time my performance was done, everybody was in tears and they gave me a standing ovation. I folded my hands in gratitude and thanked them. It was the first time that I had made people cry. That is the second most cherished feeling for an actor— the ability to move people to tears. I'll share the first, the most precious feeling, later in the story.

In no time, the entire school knew about my performance, and finally, I felt seen, like I had carved a space for myself in their world. After all this time, I had finally mustered the courage to confront my inner self and reclaim the self-belief I had lost. I felt more attuned with myself—my decisions, my vices, and my woes. Whatever state I found myself in—emotionally, socially, or otherwise—I embraced it because I finally sensed that I was growing into the person I was meant to be. It's always easier to descend from the top of a hill to its bottom; gravity's pull accelerates the fall. But to defy that gravity and climb back up requires far greater effort. Never underestimate where you stand, and always remember that every moment, no matter how challenging or painful, is as vital as any other. After all, we learn more from our failures than our successes. Failing to grasp this truth is the only failure that acts as an anti-teacher, leaving us stuck in its meaningless void.

A few days later, I was sitting in class with my hair tied neatly in a ponytail when a teacher walked in and sat behind me.

She tapped me on the shoulder and said, "Tie your hair in a braid!"

Surprised, I turned around politely and asked, "I thought my hair was neat. Is there something wrong with this hairstyle?"

To my shock, the teacher got incredibly upset and scolded me in front of the entire class for answering back. Embarrassed, I apologised right away. But I couldn't help feeling confused, my question had been polite.

Looking back, I realise my hair had always been a sensitive subject for me. This small incident lingered in my mind because it made me realise something deeper. This place wasn't for me. No matter how hard I tried to fit in, I couldn't see myself wanting to come to school. The goal of IIT I had set before joining suddenly felt like it wasn't mine. I wasn't passionate about pursuing it, and without that passion, I knew I'd never put in the effort it demanded.

Like I said before, the universe works for you, not against you. By chance, my father met the headmistress of my old IB school. During their conversation, she mentioned that they would be happy to have me back. My father told me about it and left the decision to me, whether to stay where I was or return to my old school. After some thought, I decided to go back and give MIT another shot. Without our dreams, we are nothing. I knew I couldn't live with myself if I didn't do everything in my power to pursue what I truly wanted.

This is the just right moment for me to share this lovely poem:

The Road Not Taken
By Robert Frost

Two roads diverged in a yellow wood,
And sorry, I could not travel both.
And be one traveler, long I stood
And looked down one as far as I could
To where it bent in the undergrowth;

Then took the other, as just as fair,
And having perhaps the better claim,
Because it was grassy and wanted wear;
Though as for that, the passing there
Had worn them really about the same,

And both that morning equally lay
In leaves no step had trodden black.
Oh, I kept the first for another day!
Yet knowing how way leads on to way,
I doubted if I should ever come back.

I shall be telling this with a sigh
Somewhere ages and ages hence:
Two roads diverged in a wood, and I—
I took the one less traveled by,
And that has made all the difference.

I want you to understand that this was not caused by the hair, the theatre, the no-movement campus, and not even the orthodox approach. When I sat down to logically review things, I realised that these were mere instances that triggered my thought process to take another road. One that I wanted to walk on and see. Another road that confirmed to me that the road I was on was just right. All I needed was strong self-belief. I walked on that road to find my inner strength so that I could embrace the journey that is life, with all its ups and downs, and to realise that each challenge brings with it a different view of myself.

So yes, I am back to where I belong! I don't know what the future holds for me, but I am thrilled to be chasing my goals today. Who knows whether I'll get into MIT or not, but one thing is certain: I will know that I tried my best. I did everything I could and more, and that in itself, will be enough. I stand stronger, braver, clearer, and more determined, and that is a huge victory!

I learned to embrace the art of fitting in with those who are nothing like me, finding beauty in the spaces where our differences meet. I learned the strength of staying grounded, knowing I am destined for a long and luminous journey, where dreams will rise and goals will be conquered. I learned the quiet power of working tirelessly each day, carrying forward the values that urge us to persevere, no matter what. I discovered the magic of community, of standing together, shoulder to shoulder because none of us can thrive alone.

And most importantly, I realised that there's a spark within each of us, a light uniquely our own, making us radiant in our imperfections. It is that spark that defines beauty, that breathes life into the mundane, and that, I think, is what romanticism is all about.

It's time to tell you about the most precious feeling an actor can experience. It is the joy of making someone laugh. Comedy, the hardest genre to master, is a true test of an actor's craft, and to succeed in it is nothing short of magic. While I'm far from mastering it, I believe there's an actor within all of us, capable of bringing laughter to the people we love—or at the very least, to ourselves. Life is filled with imperfections. It is a series of chaotic, messy moments. Yet, it's that inner actor in us who can find shards of happiness even in the darkest times and turn them into laughter. And that's the secret to romanticism—just laugh. Sometimes, a simple laugh can paint the world in brighter hues. It can make the grass seem greener, the skies prettier, and life itself a little kinder.

You never truly grasp the control you have over your life and the power of your choices until everything begins to crumble—and then you realise you're the only one who can rebuild it.

As Brian Tracy so aptly said, "Make your life a masterpiece; imagine no limitations on what you can be, have, or do."

I'm not just aiming for a masterpiece; I'm crafting a magnum opus—a life of purpose, resilience, and boundless possibilities. And I hope you'll do the same. Because no matter how chaotic or uncertain the road may seem, the pen is always in your hand. So, write fiercely, dream boldly, and create a life that's nothing short of extraordinary.

Manicka Kumar is a 16-year-old storyteller who is passionate about acting, art, and introspection. She blends creativity and intellect to explore life's complexities. With a love for romanticizing moments and finding meaning in everyday struggles, she inspires others to embrace their unique journeys towards happiness.

I DARE YOU TO DARE

YAMIA KHANNA

TRUE TALE 6

I Dare You to Dare

Boldness is not an innate trait; it is a deliberate choice. Once embraced, it transforms into an unparalleled source of power.

The definition of 'bold', however, can vary from person to person. For some, the colour red symbolises boldness and strength. For others, it's embodied in a sharp mind and rational thinking. On the other hand, if you're like me, you might find the ocean to be tremendously bold. When I talk about the ocean being bold, I think of its vast expanse, great depth and the ability of the waves to be completely still yet hold immense strength.

Just like the ocean, a person with deep knowledge, strong opinions and the courage to voice those opinions is, in fact, bold. A person who doesn't hold back, someone who stands up for what is right without fear of the consequences they might face— that is boldness. For me, being bold means standing firm against injustice, having zero tolerance for bullies, and always protecting those who can't protect themselves. It's about taking action when it matters most, especially when others may not have the courage to speak up.

One moment from a few years ago has stayed with me. I had a student in my class who was known for being troublesome and picking fights with others. He wasn't just a regular troublemaker; he had a sharp tongue and enjoyed making others feel small. My friend had recently lost his father, and though he was trying to keep his head up, you could see the weight of grief bearing down on him. Instead of showing him an ounce of empathy, this bully made cruel, insensitive jokes about my friend's father's death, not realising he was poking an open wound.

I saw the look on my friend's face as he froze, utterly stunned by the cruelty of it all. He was in shock, and for a brief moment, I felt his pain as if it were my own. I knew, in that instant, that I couldn't let this go. If I didn't do something, this bully would continue to prey on the vulnerabilities of others. Without a second thought, I walked over to where that boy was sitting and confronted him. I made it clear that what he had said was beyond unacceptable, that his words had not only disrespected my friend but had also wounded him deeply. I didn't shout, but my voice was firm and unwavering. I made him apologise to my friend, and I didn't stop there. I went to the principal and filed a formal complaint, demanding that the situation be addressed with the seriousness it deserved.

When my classmates saw me standing up to the bully, something shifted in the air. For the first time, they felt empowered to speak against him as well. They came forward, one by one, sharing their own experiences and grievances. Together, we stood strong, united in our belief that no one should ever be subjected to that kind of cruelty. In the end, the bully faced the consequences of his actions. That day, I learned that true boldness isn't just about confronting the wrongdoers head-on. It's about inspiring others to do the same, to help them find their own voice and stand together against injustice.

Above all, it's about supporting the vulnerable, even when it feels like you're up against the world because sometimes when you dare for someone else, you inspire that person to dare for themselves.

I don't just believe in standing up for others, but for myself too, even when the person I'm standing against seems to hold a position of higher power. I've been raised to be bold and I am thankful to my mother for this. She taught me to value myself above all, to be brave and fight against what's wrong, and to never let anyone step over me. I guess I get that boldness from her.

Oh, wait! It just dawned on me that I haven't told you much about myself! Ever since I can remember, I have loved to talk and connect with people. I'm the kind of person who enjoys learning new things. I'll have to give credit to my mother for this since she was the one who always enrolled me in all sorts of activities. I started learning how to swim at the tender age of one and a half years! My journey with sports didn't quite end there; after that, I learned how to play lawn tennis, badminton, basketball and even gymnastics, although I wasn't as successful. Out of all these sports, admittedly, swimming and basketball remain my favourites. I've made it a habit to take part in at least one swimming tournament being held in my city annually and have mostly won them, barring a few where I stood second. As for basketball, I played at the district level and bagged the second position. Unfortunately, I could not get selected for the state level. On a separate note, I enjoy baking as well, primarily because it satisfies my sweet tooth! Also, for all those wondering, I am Yamia Khanna, a 16-year-old girl who chose to walk on the road less travelled. But believe me, it wasn't all that easy!

Like everyone else, I faced my share of challenges. The difference is that I chose to not back down. I owe my resilient self to my father. He taught me that while challenges may intimidate, they are never insurmountable.

His words, "A challenge served to you is never bigger than you", have echoed in my mind during moments of doubt, reminding me to rise above fear and uncertainty.

My father lives on this philosophy every day. He does not shy away from obstacles; instead, he embraces them as personal dares. One unforgettable instance where he exhibited his resilience was when he ran a half marathon in Ladakh at an altitude of 11,155 feet. Breathing at such heights is a struggle. Yet he defied the odds and pushed himself through adverse conditions that most would find impossible to face. When he first took up long-distance running, many friends and even the family doubted him. They warned him that it would be too hard, especially given his severe lower back injury. Doctors had once advised him to quit badminton to avoid worsening his condition. It would have been easy for him to give in to self-doubt and walk away. But my father didn't let these stumbling blocks define him. Instead, he viewed these challenges as opportunities. He faced the situation with grit and determination, looked at the practical side, focused on making things happen, and triumphed brilliantly.

I watched him through this journey very closely. It was not easy, but his focus, determination, and never-say-die spirit turned challenges into triumphs. His courage and resilience cast their glow on me. His resilient personality has nourished my soul and shaped the fearless ME.

Through observational learning, I started drafting my own lessons. Firstly, 'challenges don't define you, YOU define YOU.' I understood that when you find yourself doubting your decisions or feeling unsupported, you need to take a moment to pause and reflect. Don't see a challenge as an immovable boulder; instead, think of it as a puzzle to solve or a dare to conquer.

Ask yourself, "What if I succeed?"

Secondly, "Always prepare with intention."

Failing to plan is planning to fail. Create a strategy that's logical and well thought out. And not to forget, always have a plan B. A backup option ensures that even if the first approach falters, you're not left defeated. All of this is exactly what my father did. When he decided to take on the Ladakh half marathon, he approached it with careful preparation and unwavering determination. Reaching the location a few days before the event, he allowed himself time to rest and acclimatise to the high altitude. Instead of rushing in unprepared, he kept his options realistic and rational. Once acclimatised, he began training with short runs, testing his limits and gaining a clearer understanding of how to approach the big day. It was this meticulous planning, combined with his resolve, that enabled him to face the challenge and succeed. His intention to succeed made him prepare better. Since then, whenever I feel overwhelmed by challenges, I start focusing on the intention behind the task. It is then that I find myself preparing much better.

His journey proved a vital truth, the battle is half won when you choose not to back down and the other half is fought with effort, discipline, and hard work. The most powerful takeaway for me was: don't let your challenges overpower you or allow the fear of failure to take control. That is what being daring is all about. To rise above that fear, to stand up, and face your obstacles with courage and firm intent. It is one of the boldest and most transformative things one can do.

Finally, remember that challenges are opportunities in disguise. They push you to grow, to discover strengths you didn't know you had, and to achieve what once seemed impossible. Every challenge you face is a step closer to becoming the best version of yourself. Imagine, if my father had given up and listened to all that other people had to say. What if he had not reached the location earlier than others and tested the grounds? What if he had given up before trying? What if he did not dare? Well, if he hadn't, then I would not have either. I have gained my strength and ability to dare by watching him do daring things, mindfully. He was not heedless or unsafe about his actions. He dared to do it sensibly and that is what I understand daring as.

It is not just me, all of us have some fear or another. These fears prevent us from being the best versions of ourselves. I, like many others, have stage fright. The tricky part is that I love performing—whether it's giving a speech, leading a debate, or singing (yes, I sing too!).

Whenever I step onto the stage, no matter how well-prepared I am, I start thinking about everything that could go wrong and become hyper-aware of all the eyes on me. This happens because I let fear take control of my thoughts.

Come, let's meet 11-year-old Yamia, who took part in a solo singing competition for the very first time. I remember clearly that the competition was held at my school, with five guest contestants coming from another school. There were about thirty solo contestants and I was one of the youngest performers. The entire school was invited to attend the competition. In short, there was a huge crowd.

As soon as everyone settled in, our principal welcomed the judges. Then it was time for the first performer to come up on the stage. As my turn approached, I grew increasingly nervous. My stomach started churning, and I could feel my palms sweating. The fourth performer was called upon, and as soon as she went up on the stage, I remember a teacher approached me hurriedly and informed me that I had been pushed ahead, from the seventh to the fifth position as the two performers who were supposed to go before me had backed out. That is when my fear really kicked in. It was as if my heart was sprinting at the speed of 100 kilometres an hour. I could feel a sharp sting in my stomach, and the next thing I heard was a thunderous round of applause for the girl who had just finished her performance.

A second later, I heard someone call my name, and every other sound was tuned out. My gaze faltered, and everything changed into a shapeless blur. My breathing quickened, shallow and urgent as if the air itself had grown thicker and heavier, making it hard for me to breathe normally. It was as though my very being recoiled, my skin quivering with a thousand tiny pinpricks of unease, and a shiver ran through me. I felt like my body was being held captive by my mind. It wasn't just my body that trembled; my mind became a tempest. I could feel my fear clawing at me, its grip tightening with each passing second, yet beneath that overwhelming surge, I knew the depth of my preparation. Every ounce of sweat and every moment of sacrifice that had led me to this point. I could taste the desperation to succeed, a fire burning fiercely in my chest, fighting against the suffocating shadows of doubt.

I was left with only a handful of choices, each heavy with consequences. Option one was to retreat, to withdraw like the other two performers, surrendering to the weight of fear. Option two was to walk up to the judges and beg for a chance to perform last, to postpone the inevitable and shield myself a little longer. But the final option, the one that seemed both terrifying and liberating, was to step onto that stage right then, to confront my fear head-on, just like my daring father! If you were ever in such a situation, what would you have done? Like me, would you have felt that all was lost too, and that the world was coming to a grinding halt?

At that moment, a thought pierced through the storm of doubt, "What if I did well?"

The question was like a challenge, a dare that echoed through my veins, urging me to step on the stage. I could clearly feel and visualise what my father would have done in a situation like this. And when I did, I intentionally poured every ounce of myself into that performance. The reward was unimaginable. The crowd erupted into a thunderous roar of applause; a sound so powerful that it swept all the fear from my body. So far, what my father had done was only a concept to me. This situation made me take up the dare in real time, just like him.

That competition made me realise how often we focus on the worst possible outcome and defeat. We forget to dare and to intentionally focus on all the things that could go right. Our fear makes us feel weak and incapable, even though we know how much effort we've put into preparing for the task at hand. We let doubt overshadow the strength we've built through hard work. Once you dare yourself to face that fear, it does not scare you as much the next time around.

While we're on the topic of daring yourself to face your fears, one strategy that has always worked wonders for me is the concept of 'self-talk.' Trust me, it's like magic for the mind. If you've ever read articles or watched interviews with elite athletes, you'll know they often credit a good, encouraging pep talk to themselves as a key to their success before competing. Self-talk is, quite simply, a conversation with yourself. It's about reinforcing your strengths, reminding yourself of your capabilities, and tricking your mind into believing that you are in control. This shift in mindset is powerful—it creates a mentality where you see yourself as capable, prepared, and strong. Once you internalise that belief, the fear starts to fade, and even the most intimidating tasks seem conquerable.

Imagine this: You're about to appear for an important exam. You've studied hard and are well-prepared, but as soon as you enter the exam hall, nerves take over. You overhear your friends discussing concepts, and suddenly, you feel like you've forgotten everything. Anxiety creeps in, and self-doubt starts whispering in your ear.

Then, in those tense moments before the exam begins, you should take a deep breath and say, "I can do this," "I've got this," and "I've prepared well."

Instantly, you feel a surge of confidence, a clarity that steadies your mind and prepares you to tackle the challenge head-on. This is the power of self-talk! It's not just about calming your nerves; it's about cultivating self-belief, and that's where the real magic lies. Self-belief transforms your approach to challenges. It helps you shift from focusing on potential failure to visualising success. This mindset encourages boldness and resilience, making you more willing to take risks and seize opportunities.

Self-talk is a skill that can be honed over time. The more you practise affirming your abilities, the more confident you become. This practice enables you to trust yourself, even when external circumstances seem daunting. Ultimately, self-talk leads to self-belief and self-belief fuels boldness. A person with an unwavering belief in their own abilities becomes unstoppable. Such people are not afraid to take on challenges, big or small, because they trust their strength and resilience. This is the incredible power of self-talk; it doesn't just help you face your fears; it empowers you to conquer them!

When we talk about 'bold', a pressing question tickles my mind. Is it always strong and bold or can it also be gentle *and* bold? Can the gentle and bold be daring? Does boldness always mean being unyielding, resolute, and strong or can it also stem from the quiet power of compassion, empathy, and love? For me, the answer is clear—boldness is not confined to strength alone. Boldness resides equally in the heart of someone who dares to feel deeply, care unconditionally, and love fiercely. It took me some time to understand this. Like so many, I once equated boldness with being tough and invincible. But a single, fleeting moment changed that belief forever.

It happened at an airport as my family and I were heading to our gate for a flight. Amid the chaos of the hurrying travellers,

I saw an elderly woman struggling to push her trolley up a ramp. She looked exhausted, while the world around her simply moved on. People paused, stared, and then walked away. Something in her quiet struggle called out to me. Without a second thought, I rushed to help her. As I gently pushed her trolley up the ramp, she looked at me with a mix of gratitude and surprise. She thanked me softly, her voice trembling with emotion.

But it was what she said next that stayed with me. "You're so bold," she said. I was taken aback. Curious, I asked her what she meant. Her reply was like a light piercing through the fog of my understanding. "It's not the act that was bold. It was the compassion and care that moved you to act. That's what makes you bold."

Her words echoed in my mind during the entire flight. What about you? Do you see boldness as something that must always be loud and unshakeable, or do you find strength in moments of quiet vulnerability? What I had seen as a small, unremarkable act, was extraordinary for her. Not because of the strength it took to push the trolley but because of the courage it took to care. At that moment, I understood that boldness isn't just about standing tall in the face of fear; it's about kneeling when someone else needs you. It's about baring your heart when the world tells you to shield it.

Boldness doesn't always roar. Sometimes, it whispers in the quiet acts of kindness that go unnoticed. To be vulnerable in a world that demands we hide behind masks of invincibility—that is boldness in its truest, most beautiful form.

As we near the conclusion of my story, I want to leave you with a simple yet transformative request—take a moment to confront your fears. Identify them, name them, and most importantly, accept them. Why? Because the first step towards growth is recognising what holds you back. Only when you truly see your fears can you begin to conquer them, one brave step at a time.

I ask you, dear reader—What is it that prevents you from becoming the best version of yourself? What is blocking your path? For me, that block was intimidation. I was intimidated by the possibility of failure and the weight of judgement. I feared letting myself and others down, and I was consumed by the haunting thought of not being good enough. I want you to reflect on your own story. Read mine, and in it, search for what is blocking you. Once you've identified it, don't stop there, find a mentor. For me, that person has been my father. He not only stood as a pillar of strength but also showed me, through his own actions, the solutions I needed to find within myself.

Now, your mentor doesn't have to be your parent. It could be a teacher who inspires you, a friend who pushes you forward, or even someone you've never met—a historical figure, an actor, or a writer whose life resonates with you. Whoever they are, let their guidance be the compass that points you towards your solution. But guidance alone is not enough. I urge you to do whatever it takes to confront and conquer your fears. Just don't give up. Fight, because surrendering may seem easier, but it comes with a far heavier price: regret.

I want to share a pivotal moment from my journey. While ideating with my mentor, she asked me a question that completely reframed my perspective.

She said and I quote, "What would you have done had you not dared to face your fears and followed the bold path?"

That single question hit me like a lightning bolt. It made me realise the magnitude of what was at stake.

Had I chosen to step back, to give in to my fears, I wouldn't have become who I am today. I would be a shadow of myself—perhaps functional but incomplete. That unfulfilled possibility would have been a weight on my shoulders that I would carry forever.

Now, I turn that same question over to you. What would you lose if you let your fears win? Who would you become if you never took that bold step forward? Take your time with this. Really think about it. When you find the answer, you will realise that the only thing standing between you and the life you dream of is the courage to dare.

So, I leave you with this: dare to be bold. Dare to dare. Dare to take that first step. Do not worry about being loud and daring. If a soft dare works for you, so be it. Strength isn't always loud. Sometimes, it's a quiet power that isn't so obvious to the world.

As they say, "Life is either a daring adventure or nothing. Boldness doesn't mean being rude, obnoxious, loud, or disrespectful. Being bold is being firm, sure, confident, fearless, daring, strong, resilient, and not easily intimidated."

I watched my father dare and I strapped on my shoes too. Remember, when you dare to dare, you change the game, first for yourself and then for those who are watching.

Yamia Khanna is a 16-year-old who is passionate about travelling, romcoms, and the beach. If she could, she would live at a beach resort forever. Baking is like therapy for her, especially because it satisfies her sweet tooth. Sports give her joy. Swimming and many other sports keep her energized.

TRUE TALE 7

CANCEL THE NOISE, UNAPOLOGETICALLY

RIA MEHTA

Cancel the Noise, Unapologetically

A confessional is a box, cabinet, booth, or stall where the priest in the church sits to hear the confessions of penitents. Don't be misled—I am not writing about any spiritual inclinations. Rather, I want to start with a confession.

Mentally, I have placed myself in the scenario explained above. Now, if you can picture it, let me begin. This morning, I had a falling out with my mentor about whether I should write this chapter, sharing details about my life that even my journal hasn't accessed. I was stubborn, not because I didn't want to write—I love to write—but because I didn't want to be misunderstood, judged, or gossiped about. Funny how this chapter is centred around exactly that!

We deliberated, spoke logically, sat on it, listed the pros and cons, and here we are. My mentor, an ace negotiator, convinced me to share a leg of my journey.

This journey has been one of pitfalls, turbulent waters, roadblocks and crosswinds, but also whimsical stops, wanderlust wonders and delightful roadside amusements. Foot on the throttle? Let's zip ahead!

Enjoying the journey while savouring each and every moment, even when it is arduous, is something I have learned from my Dadu—my grandfather. He was a serial explorer with a bag full of serendipitous experiences over his life's odyssey. This is what fuels my existence and very being.

A photographer by profession, he was gifted with the ability to view life through a lens and a pair of matchless blue-grey irises that even sources of creation could not give to anyone else. Truly one of a kind, my Dadu was a quiet explorer, a minimalist at heart, and a keen seeker of wisdom. His gentle smile radiated a sweetness that seemed to light up the entire room, and his twinkling eyes, framed by his black-rimmed glasses, carried a lifetime of wisdom, care, and generosity. With his neatly combed white hair and charming moustache, he embodied a sense of grace and dignity. Listening to him speak was like hearing a lullaby of kindness, each word soft yet filled with meaning. He was famously known for his art of telling stories with his camera.

His passing six years ago, just four days before my birthday, still makes me uneasy. My eyes are watery as I type this on my laptop sitting at a coffee shop, pretending that everything is fine. Soon, you'll see just how talented a performer I truly am. I still haven't warmed up to it, maybe because I do not enjoy a world without him. It would be unfair if I said he did not prepare me to deal with the unexpected twists along the journey of life. He did. Through his wisdom, he taught me patience, showing me that while life's journey can be unpredictable, staying calm and composed allows one to better handle its challenges. He also instilled resilience, sharing stories of overcoming adversity and reminding me that setbacks are temporary and a part of one's growth.

Dadu was an adventurer who had spent most of his life travelling. The first leg was a hard one, from Lahore to Delhi, during the partition. Dadu shared how he had always maintained his calm demeanour while the screams of violence, crying, wailing, and sounds of warfare, gunshots, and explosions were loud enough not to be missed. And when I look back at how he silenced these noises, I recollect how he cancelled almost every unwanted noise around him. He would move away from all the noise, be silent and would draw strength and peace from within himself.

He used his love and passion for adventure and love for the camera to channel his emotions beautifully through his photographs. My Dadu had travelled across India numerous times, and his experiences were tea-time anecdotes which everyone looked forward to listening to and learning from!

While travelling, all of us experience noises that stay persistent through all the modes, they bring chaos and jarring turbulence. In life's journey, noise—judgement, unwelcome opinions, and negativity—is inescapable, much like the cacophony of travel. Ironically, my mentor and I were discussing my chapter on noise cancellation at CCD (Café Coffee Day) on a beautiful sunny morning. The café was noisy with steam hissing from the espresso machine and people constantly walking in and out. There was commotion all around. The manager was constantly typing on the system with her long and spiky nails. It was really disturbing, but all this background noise did not distract us from the purpose of our meeting! Our inner voices made their way through the commotion, chaos, constant chatter, and all the fuss. "Ah!" I exclaimed. No wonder science could sense the need for noise-cancellation headphones! Necessity is truly the mother of invention. It struck me that if we can cancel out all the noise to focus on a conversation and enjoy some hot chocolate, why don't we do that in life with all the blabbermouths?

Did you know that the process of sound cancellation uses tiny microphones to listen to the ambient noise around you? Then the electronics in the device create a sound that is the exact opposite of that sound wave, cancelling it out so that all you hear is the music coming from your headphones—not any external sounds. Since I travel frequently from home to Bangalore for college, I have noticed that people usually wear huge headphones to cancel out those annoying background noises. And I don't blame them! Well, the point of educating you on the science of noise cancellation is that my Dadu did that. He did just that! Without any technology, he cancelled all the creators of negative impact around him, whether it was people, things or situations. He simply heard the music, the happy music of life.

As a child, I can't say when I clearly noticed and absorbed that. Today, I fully comprehend and appreciate it. The journey I am going to take you on in this chapter is about how I learned the power of noise cancellation in real life, just like my Dadu. How I identified the difference between music and noise. The fact that music is pleasant, while noise is an unwanted sound, one that must be nullified. I also want to take you through the moments when I couldn't distinguish between the two, when I got caught in the noise, and how it impacted me, and ultimately led to the need for cancellation.

My life while growing up was rather wholesome and harmonious with a few minor bumps along the way. These temporary stumbling blocks did not make me pause for a break but kept the journey entertaining, especially with my co-passengers, my mom and dad! I'd rather call them the drivers, tour guides, and travel agents of this beautiful journey. Their innate tendencies of patience, supportiveness, discipline, and sacrifice along with severe protocols ensured that my brother and I had a mellow ride. They were my anchors and made sure the ship of my life was parked at the harbour and also sailing when the weather was right. They were beacons of kindness, radiating positivity, and gracefully entertaining. They wore their hearts on their sleeves and walked with integrity, unfazed by others' actions.

With big, bright, and curious eyes, I was always full of energy as a child, eager to explore the world around me. My curiosity and enthusiasm for life have been constant, driving me to learn, discover, and embrace every experience with a sense of wonder. I was living in my own world, full of love, great food, and lots of fun without a care about what anyone else felt, thought or said. Now, I rewind the clips of the 12-year-old Ria living life to the fullest, jumping and exploring the world as if she owns it, without a worry. It made me realise that I had so much confidence in who I was, I loved who I was but also made me think that I was living in a bubble where everyone was sweet. I did not bother about what anyone would think of me. However, this was soon disproved by the universe!

The bubble of my whimsical childhood was floating in a playground of imagination, fuelled by pure joy and limitless creativity until it all went downhill. The bubble was popped by people with long and pokey noses with baseless opinions, rather than judgement. These opinions were about me, my parents, my upbringing, and the lifestyle I led. There were many backhanded comments, rumours, judgemental stares, and taunts that embarrassed and humiliated me. What was agonising was the fact that I received most of this treatment from people I called 'friends.'

They had painted an image of me—one that bore no resemblance to the real me. Yet, the painting was so boldly projected that somehow, I became labelled and identified by this hideous and completely contrasting image. One that was anything but me. What could I have done? I wasn't painting this image—they were! I wasn't providing the inputs for this image—they were assuming things! They judged, interpreted, and simply painted it! And, in today's terms, that image went viral.

This erroneous, inaccurate, false, misleading, invalid, untrue, distorted, and utterly inexact image became the subject of everyone's gossip. This image did not look like me, walk like me, or even speak like me. She was my antithesis, to say the least. The source and origin of this image? Unknown.

Suddenly, I was being judged for the way I carried myself. My persona became the subject of relentless discussion. Everything I did was scrutinised—whether it was participating in extracurricular activities or balancing academics alongside my (fake) social circle.

It was astonishing and truly mind-blowing how a girl—me—who had done nothing wrong was suddenly being mercilessly trolled and viciously teased simply because of how her parents had raised her.

To understand the futility of their judgement, you must first know what their opinions were. Only then will the baselessness of it all become clear.

The label? A 'spoilt rich brat'! (Please imagine a hundred exclamation marks here because I was everything BUT that!)

If you haven't already donned the judgemental hat while reading this, you would see that I was leading a normal life. A life full of love and protection, of being provided with the best, and simply being cherished as the apple of my family's eye—be it my parents or grandparents. I was deeply loved. The love, care, and attention I received built my self-esteem, NOT MY EGO. The warm, loving family relationships made me feel valued and worthwhile, not spoilt. My family's rituals gave me a sense of belonging, not pampering. Trying new things made me feel confident, NOT PRIVILEGED.

Everything I received from my family was couched in a positive light—one that was supposed to illuminate my perspective, exposure, self-esteem, and confidence. Anyone who has grown up in a family with grandparents around would appreciate that the child is always kept grounded. The child is loved, sometimes even pampered, yet always reminded of the humble roots, the struggles, the realities, and the rising-from-nowhere journey. Our bedtime stories revolved around how we once had nothing, worked hard, and became who we were today. We were never told, "Here is your silver spoon, go conquer the world."

And that was what hurt the most. I came from a family that valued their journey, struggles, losses, and achievements. Had that not been so, I would not have been writing this chapter!

'You see what you want to see' is a phrase that suggests that our perceptions are influenced by our beliefs, desires, and expectations. They are not governed by those of the person you are judging. However, this is the sensibility I have now. At that moment, these external perceptions felt like nothing short of a swamp that kept pulling me in every time I moved. The sheer cruelty and unjust judgements were like a tidal wave of negativity crashing down upon me with force. Funny how all of it was based on nothing but the ignorant assumptions of some callous people. That was indeed a nightmare for a 12-year-old girl, who was actually content and satisfied in her beautiful world.

It felt like nothing short of something straight out of a movie. The ordeal flipped my life completely. Like a whirlwind, this started transforming things around me in ways I never imagined possible. I felt miserable. I no longer recognised the people I had been calling my friends for three years. There was so much noise and chatter around me. I felt lost in my own school and because of this dissonance between the image projected by others and my true self, I even felt lost at home.

My mentor told me about the phrase "Nobody puts Baby in a corner." It was a line from her favourite movie from 1987, 'Dirty Dancing.' It refers to someone being ignored or unfairly excluded. It implies that the person deserves to be recognised for their abilities or talents and not judged for the same. However, at that moment, Baby was put in a corner—and so was I.

In fact, I was put into a box based on my looks and my fashion sense. Everyone had built perceptions of me in their heads. My love for fashion and dressing up bothered them far more than it did me. They assumed that they had the creative liberty to assign labels to me. They called me superficial or materialistic just because I loved dressing up and going out, but they didn't understand the full picture. Being labelled as 'shallow' and an 'attention seeker' really made me question my worth. I was misunderstood by the people I thought knew me inside out.

Being judged for my looks and external attributes really made me ask myself, "Am I really who they think I am?"

I was 12. I was in a swamp. I was crowded by assumptions. I started questioning the validity of my self-belief. The fact that I vividly remember who said what and when even seven to eight years later shows the lasting impact of words carelessly thrown at me. I was bitterly disappointed and devastated by the deceit. I was pushed off a cliff by my so-called best friends, and I was lost in a sea of confusion and hurt. Instead of standing up for me and cheering for me, my friends spoke ill of me and brought me down.

As I pieced together the key details of the chatter that suddenly surrounded me—in class, on the playground, and in the art room, I got to know that I was being underestimated. After all those continuous prizes I won, competitions I participated in, and A pluses I got right since grade 1, these gossip mongers suddenly felt that I was incapable of achieving anything in life. All they felt was that I would like to score a Hermès Birkin Bag rather than a 95% in my board exams.

I wonder why? Why give me all that attention? Why not find something better to do? Why not find something creative or worthwhile? Why not remove the limelight from me? But of course, these questions were in my head; I never posed any of these questions to them.

I did not know that one could get bullied for their hobbies and leisure activities. This criticism around wearing good clothes and also getting great grades was, in fact, used to make me feel inadequate in every sense. I doubted myself, my choices, and even my simple hobby of looking at fashion magazines. I could never have anticipated the kind of exclusion and isolation I was subjected to.

Ironically, this situation made me shine as a great performer! I was always moving around with a big smile on my face while I was completely shattered on the inside. I must try my hand at the theatre too!

Growing up, I had full attendance at school; I would not take any days off throughout the year. But during this phase, I had to force myself to get out of bed, get ready, and head to school. From the moment I stepped into the school premises until the bell rang at the end of the day, I had to force myself to exist. Once I came back after a dull day, I would mentally prepare myself to go back the next day. It felt as if I was going to war every single day. Staying at home was also becoming a struggle, as the feeling of being misjudged at school always stayed with me.

I had stopped talking to my two close friends. I felt completely lost, with no sense of direction. I had no other choice but to fake a smile every day and behave normally. I hoped to smile from within one day. Oh! I dreamt of it every single day, I yearned for it. This situation disrupted my sense of identity and left me feeling bewildered.

On one hand, people assumed I only aspired to own Hermès bags. On the other, some expected me to score 99%! Why they thought I would leave that 1% for someone else is beyond me. These unrealistic expectations caused constant stress, anxiety, and burnout. I began procrastinating and my studies suffered, distracted by all the noise around me. I lost all the belief that I had in myself. I was so consumed by what everyone thought about me that it shattered my confidence. I started drawing back from extracurriculars, avoided going to my evening classes, and lost touch with everyone around me. In my two decades of existence, nothing compares to the criticism I faced between the ages of 12 and 17.

In this journey of life, a bridge had to be crossed. A bridge that none of my drivers or family were aware of. A bridge that was not mentioned in the itinerary. The bridge swayed ominously in the wind, its rusted beams creaking like the groans of an ancient creature. With each step, the wooden planks jolted beneath my feet, as if reluctant to bear my weight.

And then, one fine day, I woke up feeling different!

The words that kept spinning in my head were—IT IS NOT A FACT!

I realised that feeling judged was an internal experience. It was a feeling, not a fact.

It was a feeling, not a fact. IT WAS NOT A FACT. And I was suddenly done! Done with all the baseless judgement. Done with others questioning my intelligence and beliefs. DONE. PERIOD.

It was time to cross over. I began to realise that not all judgement serves you and that it was not fair to let random people's judgement ruin your happiness. With repeated contemplation and introspection, I understood that feeling judged and being judged is not the same thing! There is a clear and important distinction. And understanding this can make the difference between feeling insecure or stable. It was the difference between hiding and shining.

I understood that how I felt and reacted to others was up to me. I may be triggered by what someone said. I was judging myself based on someone's words, actions, a certain look, or a sneering sound under their breath—these were external things, and I could either react to them or not. And right there, I made a choice—to not accept it. I decided to cross that bridge all by myself with no strong ropes holding the bridge and no sturdy handles to grasp. I was determined to cross over, with my chin up.

As an extrovert, I loved talking to people. I learned to push past the heartache, stay true to my focus, and stand up for myself. I promised to be braver and come through this situation until I did not have to fake a smile everywhere I went.

This became my top priority, and I set a goal for myself to be truly happy so it automatically showed on my face. I wanted to glow from inside and be in a state of bliss. I dreamt of the day with my eyes wide open. I wanted to be respected for who I was instead of being looked down upon. Without a need for any validation, I wanted to attain the power to believe in myself and embrace myself as I was.

So why did I choose to relive this very painful phase of my life, today, in this chapter?

So you don't ever have to!

Here are my two cents:

From what I have gathered, the first step is clearing away the distractions if you want to realise your dreams. Set boundaries by analysing what works for you and what does not. You also need to set clear boundaries with people who do not respect your time, bring you down, do not value your presence, or judge you. Mindfulness is key. The primary focus is to master 'the art of saying no.' Realising what you are worth and what you bring to the table is what makes all the difference.

Remember, it's a feeling, not a fact. I stopped going to places where I was not respected. I completely cut out those who gossiped about me. I only went with the uplifters! I connected with things that brought me sanity and made me feel better.

Gradually, as my confidence and belief in myself grew, I started trusting myself more. The noise faded into the background as I moved forward with clarity. There were days when I doubted myself, when the constant chatter around me felt overwhelming. But I found strength in calmness.

Quietly but firmly, I fought back. I could feel the birth of an unshakeable resilience.

I began to realise that the only opinion that mattered was my own.

A five-step approach got me through. I remember it as clearly as a sticky note in my head:

1. Identifying the source of noise: As Nikhil Kamath has mentioned, "Make a list of all the drama that happens and people who cause that drama in your life, eliminate the people who create the drama." My additional suggestion would be to inspire them to enrol in theatre classes. In my head, I had laid out the names of the noise creators and eliminated them. Not only out of sight but also out of mind. It took time, but I did it.

2. Setting clear boundaries and sticking to them regardless of how hard it is. I ensured I did not give in to any temptation of going back to them in the moments they were nice or inviting or when they wore the mask of 'being friends.'

3. Crafting a clear plan to achieve mental clarity, peace of mind, and goals. Yes! I had a plan on how to avoid noise creators, stay quiet, stay away, behave in public, which events to miss, and how to occupy myself constructively.

4. Practice mindfulness by focusing on the here and now, being aware of what is happening in the present moment, rather than being lost in past memories or future worries. This was tough! I was often reminded of what they had done, and obviously, my brain asked why. Repeatedly, with every contemplation, there were no answers. So, I stuck to my answer. This is not a fact. I shall not accept it.

5. Reflect on yourself regularly by practising the process of evaluating your life and actions to better understand who you are and how you can grow. Writing a journal, contemplating, self-talk and the determination to cross the bridge were my methods of reflection.

I started spending more time alone, creating a healthy space for self-discovery, growth, and rejuvenation. It led to a more fulfilled, centred, and independent life. It helped me reconnect with my inner self, accentuating my improved mental health, creativity, and a stronger sense of purpose. I was becoming happy again.

Just as my Dadu taught me, 'our greatest achievement comes not from proving others wrong, but from proving to ourselves what we are capable of .' That is exactly what I did.

While walking on that treacherous bridge all by myself, taking support and motivation from the guides I am blessed with, following the universe's casting light, I found the direction and path to my goal.

The triumph of any tale depends on consistency. Our ability to surpass obstacles consistently over a period of time. I want to share that today, as I turn twenty-one and relive my life as a teenager, I can confirm that I have been consistently living on this path of realisation by being irrelevant to the noise around me.

Today I raise a toast to the noise cancellation my 16-year-old self-created. I heard the music of the unstoppable power and unbreakable hope that wanted me to break free from all the things that were pulling me down.

I realised noise cancellation was my game-changer!

It is truly the ability to nullify any distraction, opinion, or judgement that pulls one down. Noise cancellation to me means being able to focus on the music, to be able to listen to it and to walk on my path towards my goal.

Easier said than done, it took me more than three years to learn to do this.

I hope this chapter helps you understand the importance of identifying the noise in your life and making all the possible efforts towards cancelling it. This is not an easy journey. It is a journey of mixed emotions, constant defeats and endless efforts to stand up again. It annoys you, unsettles you and no number of guides and agents can help you get out of it until you decide to.

It takes an immense amount of courage and mindfulness to identify the constant chatter and noise around all of us. All it needs is courage and grit to say that I shall not accept this.

It is when you take a stance for yourself, believing in what you are, that you can reach the stage where the music flows clearly in your ears.

All you have to do is shut out the noise and listen to yourself. Decide what you need, and what is good for your true self, and then go get it unapologetically.

Quoting from 'And Still I Rise' by the legendary Maya Angelou.

"You may kill me with your hatefulness,

But still, like air, I'll rise."

The world has repeatedly attempted to shatter me. Using every insult to make me feel inferior, people have attempted to hurt me with their harsh remarks. I've seen their scornful, icy gazes pierce me as though I don't belong. They made an effort to obliterate me and make me feel unimportant and unworthy. But no matter what, I rise. Because I am not what they say I am. I am not their judgement or their hatred. I am my own strength, my own voice, my own spirit. I rise because they can't hold me down. And no matter how many times they try to bury me, I will always rise.

Ria Mehta is a creative 21-year-old with a heart full of dreams. She finds joy in life's little moments, be it sharing stories and painting her thoughts onto a canvas, or diving into a romcom. With her love for hosting, her infectious energy, and her passion for helping others, she effortlessly creates connections and turns ordinary moments into cherished memories.

About the Curator

Chhavii Mehtaa is an educator and mentor by profession. She is the author of *Conscious Parenting: Nurturing Hearts, Shaping Future*, which continues to inspire parents worldwide. Motivated by her passion for storytelling, she founded the Young Authors Launchpad and The Voice Masters Club—platforms that empower children to express their unique ideas, develop their writing skills and cultivate self-belief.

Her collaborations include working with Turkey's Ministry of Culture and Tourism on a children's book. She is also the recipient of the prestigious Dr. Sarojini Naidu International Award for Working Women 2024, presented by the ICMEI (International Chamber of Media & Entertainment Industry) and International Women's Film Forum for her dedicated efforts and inspiring impact on the community.

Recognised as one of Today's Fifty Under 50 Inspiring Women, Chhavii has also been featured in magazines like Literary Mirror and Perfect Woman. As part of the New Age MomPreneurs community, she connects with other mothers to share strategies for managing entrepreneurship and family life.

Chhavii is a firm believer in self-care and mindfulness. She finds joy in the simple pleasures of life, always keeping a book to read and a drink to sip within reach.